# TEACHING NUMERACY: A MANUAL FOR TUTORS

by

**Terry and Christine Riley**

**National Extension College, Cambridge**

Published by the National Extension College, 131 Hills Road, Cambridge.
© 1977 National Extension College Trust Ltd.
ISBN: 0 86082 113 7
All rights reserved
Set and printed by the National Extension College.
Acknowledgements: Illustrations John Holder, Photographs Tony Othen

**The National Extension College gratefully acknowledges the financial support of the Nuffield Foundation which made the production of this Manual possible.**

Reprinted 1978

**Authors**

*Terry Riley* has two first degrees, one in Philosophy and one in Education as well as a postgraduate certificate in Education. He was former County Co-ordinator for Adult Literacy with Nottinghamshire County Council and is now full time consultant with the Adult Literacy Resource Agency. He was the founder of the Nottingham Council for Voluntary Service Numeracy Project and at present chairs its Management Committee.

*Christine Riley* worked in the Civil Service prior to studying for a certificate of Education. She has subsequently worked with both children and adults specialising in the teaching of basic skills with particular reference to the design of integrated numeracy/ literacy programmes.

# CONTENTS

# Part III  Case studies

# FOREWORD

## Is innumeracy a problem?

No one knows the extent of innumeracy among adults in this country. However, there is evidence of increasing concern about the standard of mathematics among school leavers in the recent comments of many employers in the press and in the findings of the special Commons Committee investigating the educational standards of school leavers.[1]  From this evidence it is difficult to draw firm conclusions as to whether general standards of numeracy are improving or declining. But what is alarming is that in a highly technological society there are undoubtedly substantial numbers of adults who cannot perform basic operations such as those involving whole numbers, fractions and decimals. The implications of this are serious both for the individual and for society.

We all need to be fluent with basic number work to cope with the increasing mathematical demands of everyday life. Life is difficult for an adult who is unable to perform simple tasks such as checking change, or checking bills and pay slips. It is also tragic that many, because of their poor levels of numeracy, are denied access to jobs which otherwise they could fill perfectly well. The effect on the national economy is also immeasurable. Because of innumeracy many people who could benefit from training courses in colleges and the government training schemes are either denied access to them, or, if fortunate

[1] *The attainment of the school leaver.* House of Commons Paper 525, H.M.S.O. which came to the conclusion that approximately 1 in 9 of school leavers did not have the arithmetic competence of the average 11 year old.

enough to secure a place, may receive no specialist help and thus are unable to derive maximum benefit from these courses.

It is obvious that on the grounds of national well-being as well as for humanitarian reasons, adults who wish to improve their numeracy should have access to appropriate facilities. Sadly, this is not the case. Although some Adult Education Centres, Colleges of Further Education, the Training Services Agency, and voluntary organisations have provision for numeracy teaching, in very many areas nothing is being done. Even in the best, the number of places available does not reflect the true extent of the problem, but rather, the demand of those few people who have the motivation and stamina to track down a local class.

The lessons of the Adult Literacy Campaign of the last few years are highly relevant to us here. Before the national and local publicity in 1973 only some 5,000 adults were receiving tuition.[1] After the publicity and with the injection of modest funds at both national and local level, the service increased twenty-fold within the space of four years. The message is clear:

to mount a class only if sufficient people ask for one is not the way to tackle the real need for adult basic education in Britain today. It is necessary to make a positive move to recruit students and to publicise the opportunities available. Without such efforts the provision for adult numeracy will remain at its present pitiful level.

This manual is written for those tutoring, or intending to tutor, adults who experience difficulty with basic number skills. It aims to provide practical help and guidance for day-to-day, or week-to-week teaching. Numeracy

[1] Haviland, Michael, *Survey of Provision for Adult Illiteracy in England,* University of Reading, 1973.

2

tutors teach under many different conditions, some have fulltime jobs, others are paid to teach evening classes and many others work voluntarily and either teach small groups or on a one-to-one basis. Not all the contents of this manual will be equally relevant to all those concerned with adult numeracy.

Numeracy tuition also rightly falls within the concern of a variety of organisations each of which displays a distinctive ethos and mode of operation: the Adult Education Service, Colleges of Further Education, government training schemes, voluntary organisations, the penal service etc. Nevertheless, we believe there are common denominators in the work which justify a general manual such as this.

In broad terms the approach adopted is one in which numeracy is regarded as a functional ability and not as a pursuit which has value in itself. This is not to deny that particular skills need to be known by the student — on the contrary, such skills are essential, but he needs to be able to use these skills in real life. *What we suggest is, that wherever possible, the number skills should be taught in contexts relevant to the student.*

The manual is divided into three parts. The first deals with matters of organisation as well as more immediate teaching concerns. The second is a suggested progression in terms of number skills. It is *not* a syllabus or programme of work as such generalised schemes can take no account of individual needs. The final part, presented in the form of case studies, is intended to give an indication of how the teaching of basic number skills can be related to those individual needs. (They are, of course only examples and what you actually do with your student or students will reflect their particular mathematical needs as they have described them.)

# PART I   NUMERACY: THE STUDENT AND THE TUTOR

## 1.1  An introduction to numeracy

Numeracy is concerned with the development of basic computational skills within the context of the mathematical needs of the individual. Numeracy requires two abilities: first, the ability to perform certain basic mathematical calculations and understand the operations involved; and second, the ability to relate the skills involved in doing such calculations to the ordinary everyday situations in which they are needed.

Numeracy tuition is thus a lot more than the mechanical teaching of basic number skills in the abstract, for it is concerned with developing the ability to cope with the everyday mathematical demands made upon adults in our society. Such a functional approach stresses the *purpose* for which mathematical skills are needed, for there is no virtue in being able to perform calculations for their own sake. Numeracy is a skill to be used. Adults, when faced with real life problems — checking a bill, calculating overtime, or whatever — need the ability both to 'translate' the situation into mathematical operations, and to perform these operations (or to be able to use aids such as calculators).

It is equally important that the numerate adult is able to work in an *appropriate* way. Undoubtedly there is a certain amount of stigma attached to innumeracy. In many situations it is embarrassingly inappropriate for an adult to pull out pencil and paper or calculator to perform a simple mental calculation that others would do 'in their heads'. Adults need to be able to cope with such calculations mentally and at a reasonable speed. We also need to know when accuracy or when speed is of greater importance and work accordingly.

Since we are defining numeracy in functional terms, and not exclusively in terms of sub-skills, it follows that because needs vary so much from individual to individual there can be no curriculum which is equally suitable to all. Nevertheless, there are certain basic mathematical operations which the vast majority, if not all, adults need to be familiar with. Part II of this manual elaborates these computational processes, though individual students, usually for reasons connected with employment, may wish to progress much further.

Most of the everyday maths we need is at a basic level. You may find it informative to keep a 'maths diary' for a period of a week or so, in order to discover the nature of your own mathematical needs.

| Situation ie why you needed to do calculations, and where | The problem | Operation(s) involved | Size of numbers involved eg 0—20, £1—100 | Means of calculations — mental — written — calculators, etc |
|---|---|---|---|---|
| shopping in a supermarket | need to work out whether it is cheaper to buy a 5 kg packet of Soap powder than usual 1 kg size. | Find out cost of 1 kg and multiply by 5 to see if this was same as or greater than 5 kg packet | 1 - 5 kg 89p — £3.59p | mental |

An analysis of your findings (and those of other tutors) will probably reveal that a common core of skills is needed, and that the work situation provides the largest number of variations from this common core.

Norman Moore conducted an interesting investigation in 1958 of the personal, social and business usage of maths by 88 adults who represented a cross-section of the population.[1] His findings were:

- Approximately 90% used addition and subtraction of number and money regularly whereas only 45% used multiplication and division regularly.

- 45% used addition and subtraction of fractions, and only 10% multiplication and division of fractions.

- Over half of maths problems were related to money.

- Calculations involving capacity, linear measure, logs, square roots, decimals,[2] fractions, etc altogether accounted for only 5% of total problems.

The message from such findings and the subjective assessment of students' needs is clear. *All adults need a thorough working knowledge of basic number skills and relatively few need more advanced mathematical ability.*

[1] Quoted in *Maths for Life*, Norman Moore and Alec Williams, O.U.P. 1976.
[2] Admittedly, the importance of a working knowledge of decimals has increased dramatically recently with the introduction of decimalisation and metrication.

## 1.2 The adult learner

The numeracy student may have failed to acquire for one reason or another, the basic number skills while at school but this lack of knowledge of a particular set of skills must not lead us to categorise all such students on the grounds of intelligence or other distinguishing features for which there is no evidence. The dangers of adopting such all-embracing classifications can lead to patronising attitudes and inappropriate programmes of work. We trust we would never categorise those with poor knowledge of geography or biology in similar ways. Nor would we adopt set attitudes to those who admit to not being able to drive, or who are disastrous at gardening.

The numeracy student, as with all who study a body of knowledge, is an individual who brings his own particular experiences, abilities and expectations to bear on the learning process. However, as an adult, he has aspects in common with other adult learners, irrespective of the subject studied. The result of this is to make adult numeracy a very different activity from numeracy in school. Students may possess a number of the following characteristics in varying degrees.

- The student may lack concentration and be tired because he has worked all day (so may you!). If so, try to vary the type of work and limit the length of each section. Do not persevere for too long if some point is difficult to grasp. Remember to have breaks when you can both just chat.

- He may find it difficult to remember specific facts. With increasing age the ability to recall declines. Be sure to include practice in the learning programme and at the beginning of lessons recapitulate on previous work.

- He may find it difficult to learn new facts and processes. This may be because he has to unlearn errors which have become ingrained over the years, or because he is nervous about the process of learning itself. Wherever possible try to reassure and build up confidence. In all cases try to avoid adding to confusion; for example, if your student remembers how to do subtraction by equal addition then don't introduce the decomposition[1] method even though this has advantages for students new to subtraction. In general, aim to give encouragement and avoid a patronising attitude.

- He may be unforthcoming or, on the contrary, wish to spend all the time in talking to you. This may be because he is nervous; in any event try to balance sociability with doing some work.

- He will possibly have knowledge and expertise in areas in which you know relatively little. Through these you can both help to develop his self-confidence and relate his specific knowledge to mathematical concepts.

- He may have strong (possibly hidden) feelings of guilt or inadequacy deriving in part from previous maths teaching which may have been extremely authoritarian.

[1] See Part II section 2.6.1.

- He will probably have more ability than a child to relate specific learning into a broader framework. This ability should be utilised. You should encourage your student to see the interrelationships of processes and their applications. He may well present examples which are relevant to him and which can form the basis for further explanation and practice.

### General guidelines
Although it is impossible to give specific advice about particular students, we can outline a few general points which you can bear in mind when you teach.

- Be friendly without swamping your student in a false bonhomie.

- Be encouraging without being patronising. Your student may not know how to multiply 5·6 by 39·72 but that does not mean he needs to be treated as a child!

- Involve your student as much as you can by a) discussing his mathematical needs with him, b) explaining what you are attempting to do, and c) encouraging his frank responses about the work the two of you are doing.

## 1.3 The student who also has difficulty with literacy
Many students who require help with basic number work also experience difficulties with the written word. This is not altogether surprising as many of the causes are interrelated. Those, for instance, who missed much of their schooling due to ill-health are likely to have fallen behind both in their reading and their maths. Similarly, those students who strongly disliked school and dropped out in spirit, if not always bodily, were probably alienated by more than one subject. Indeed, the problem can be more acute with maths because of the sequential nature of the tasks involved. A child who is absent from school for any length of time, can find himself hopelessly lost when he returns and may never catch up unless extra efforts are made both by himself and his teacher or parents. A vicious circle can soon develop in which the child does not understand the work his class mates are doing and consequently feels himself to be stupid and the work boring. In many cases resentment sets in which can affect his whole attitude to school.

What can the tutor do if his student has difficulty with both literacy and numeracy?

- If you suspect that your student has difficulty with literacy it is important to discuss this with him. Discover also how the local literacy scheme operates and suggest he gets in touch with someone there, supplying the appropriate name, address and telephone number.

- If the student is already receiving literacy tuition it is essential that you get in touch with his literacy tutor in order to discover exactly what he can and cannot do in terms of reading and writing.

- Wherever possible joint programmes should be evolved between yourself, the literacy tutor, and of course, the student. In this way you can ensure that you present work which he can read. Moreover, by working in conjunction with a literacy worker you can also assist in the development of his literacy skills as well as his numeracy and vice versa.

- The crucial factor is that the maths work you present to your student is geared to his literacy ability. It is pointless for instance to set written problems if he cannot read the words used. Remember that this applies not only to the rather dreary problems presented in many school texts but also to real life problems, eg calculations based on timetables, wage slips, in fact anything involving words.

- Care must be taken in diagnosis so that the inability to read and write is not confused with lack of understanding of mathematical concepts. There is always the danger that a student's poor level of literacy will disguise his fluency with number concepts, and this will result in a less demanding programme of work than is necessary.

## 1.4 A balanced programme of work

The teaching approach advocated in this manual is one which stems from our belief that adult numeracy has two main aspects:

number work is sequential in nature,

that we need to be numerate for a purpose and not as an end in itself (ie that numeracy is functional).

However, each of these aspects, if given exclusive attention, can result in an unbalanced and ineffective programme of work. Thus if the various skills are taught without reference to the needs of an individual adult the work will be extremely boring, and although the student may be fluent with the operations when written down, he may not be able to translate his own mathematical problems into a numerical form. Similarly, a programme of work which concentrates exclusively on the day-to-day needs of the student is highly unlikely to cover all the sub-skills with which he may need to be familiar to to cope with his changing needs in the future.

Consequently, the ideal programme is one which both ensures that all the basic skills are taught and introduces them through the student's own particular situation. The skills are thus taught in a context which is relevant to the student. Number work, though, needs a lot of practice and this is particularly the case if the aim is speed as well as accuracy. There is no quick way to develop a student's ability to do calculations rapidly (if indeed this is a skill he needs) other than by practising. Such practice, though, should never be regarded as a substitute for the main activity in any lesson — developing a deeper understanding of mathematical concepts and operations.

To help get the balance right between the various components it is essential that you spend time planning both the programme as a whole and individual lessons.

## The necessity of planning

No matter what subject is being taught it is vitally important that the tutor plans in advance. If consideration is not given to planning, teaching sessions are at best, a hit and miss affair, and at worst an aimless exercise. *Planning should be undertaken at two levels: the total programme and the individual lesson.*

- *Planning the programme.* It is important that both you and your student know where you are going. Through consultation with your student you need to frame the broad outlines of the teaching programme bearing in mind both the sequential nature of number work (see Part II) and his particular mathematical needs. Such a programme must of necessity be tentative as it stretches into the future and will be influenced by a number of factors, including the student's changing needs and his rate of progress. However, it may be helpful if you write down the broad overview of the teaching/learning programme for the coming term even though this will not be rigidly followed in every detail.

- *Planning lessons.* It is important to plan lessons in advance, so that you know what you will be doing and have materials prepared prior to the lesson. However, any lesson plan should be flexible for points may occur during the session which should be utilised. Moreover, your student may have a real numeracy need, (eg checking a bill) which can form the basis for learning rather than the work you intended.

When structuring a lesson bear in mind the following points —

- How long will the lesson be? 1½—2 hours is usually long enough.
- Make sure there's a coffee and/or a chat in the middle.
- Break up the lesson into sections, usually not spending more than 15 or 20 minutes on each section.
- Try as far as possible to vary the nature of the sections,

eg    (a)  recapitulation of the last session with further examples.
        (b)  real life problem, eg calculating cost of food bills.

(c) developing further the skills used in (b)

**Coffee break**

(d) practice calculations.

(e) practice at applying skills learnt in (b) to new situations, eg addi-tion of meals on a menu.

Following the lesson you may find it useful to sketch out a short written plan for the following week while working within the larger framework for the forthcoming weeks and months.

Other factors which affect your lesson plan will include the following:

(a) What your student needs to know.

(b) What he has expressly stated he wishes to learn.

(c) Your aim for that particular session.

(d) Acting upon information supplied by diagnosis – how you can implement it, ie the teaching strategies you will adopt.

(e) What materials/resources you will need.

(f) Monitoring the success of the lesson.

## 1.5 The diagnosis of students' abilities

If you are effectively to help your student develop his mathematical skills it is important to know exactly what he can and cannot do so that you can gear the work to his present abilities. This is important for any subject but is crucial in developing number skills, as basic maths is sequential in nature. Much time can be wasted either by teaching at too low or too high a level. Diagnosis is the process whereby information is gathered and analysed so that appropriate teaching can take place. Moreover, by careful observation you will be able to discover more than simply the student's level of ability: for instance, what particular strengths he brings to the learning situation, and his preferred mode of learning, eg discovering for himself or receiving explanations.

Diagnosis is not an end in itself. It is only of value if the information influences your subsequent teaching. In other words, the conclusions you arrive at concerning the student's learning should be fed in to form a teaching cycle.

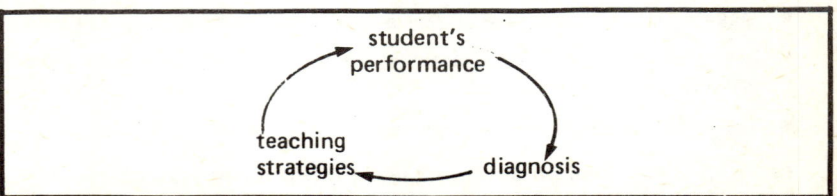

For this reason diagnosis should not be regarded as a once and for all operation, or something done every six months, but as an on-going process. Indeed in practice it may be difficult to determine where diagnosis ends and teaching begins, the two are so closely interrelated.

The two main stages in diagnosis are first to gather relevant information and second to analyse and interpret it, though, as stated above, unless the conclusions are acted upon the exercise is worthless.

● **Gathering information**

1) Observation and discussion with the student.

The most important source of information is the student himself. He alone can tell you why and what he needs to learn. Moreover, the student can explain when he fails to understand a calculation or problem, which aspects are straightforward to him and which mystifying. Thus, continual discussion between tutor and student (or groups of students) is essential. Not only do you as a tutor receive constant information about your student's work, but also it helps to develop in the student a sense of responsibility for his own learning, so breaking down the mystique of the subject and the idea that he is the passive receiver of knowledge.

Through discussion, combined with observation, you will be able to discover which broad strategies he adopts when learning and which are most effective. In order to reach conclusions, it may be helpful to consider questions such as:

● What are the student's strengths? Eg does he understand and remember more if he works from cognitive rules and explanations, or by demonstration, or by discovering a process himself?

● What type of error does he make? Eg does he fail to transfer a real problem to a written form (or onto a calculator), does he understand the operation, or are his errors due to lack of accuracy?

● What specific errors does he make? Eg does he understand the importance of place value, does he know basic number bonds?

Furthermore, through careful observation, it will be possible to record particular errors your student makes so that you can explain the points subsequently. This can be done in a notebook or by means of a simple record sheet such as:

11

| Date | Concept operation | Teaching approach | Nature of difficulties, if any | Proposed action, eg further practice or different approach |
|------|-------------------|-------------------|-------------------------------|-----------------------------------------------------------|
| 10/1/78 | Vertical Subtraction | Following on from horizontal Subtraction using labelled columns. | No serious ones, though some problems at first with place value | Will go on to multiplication but keep emphasising importance of place value by asking students to read out answers out loud. |

Whichever way you record the information, the important point is that you have some retrieval system to act as a memory aid for subsequent discussions between the student and yourself, and to act as a guide for future teaching.

The advantage of observation as opposed to formal testing is that it is an ongoing activity whereby diagnosis is an integral part of the whole teaching/ learning process.

2)    Formal diagnostic tests.

These are usually presented as a series of calculations or written problems. They undoubtedly have some advantages: they can give a quick overview of a student's abilities and thus provide information when a student commences tuition or later on give an indication of progress (if one is needed). However, they have numerous limitations, the most serious of which is that they assess only a limited range of abilities, usually the ability to answer sums or written problems (remember too that many students may have difficulties with reading written problems which may adversely influence the results). Published tests cannot cater for the real life mathematical problems which all students need to cope with. Tests may also produce a state of tension in the student possibly resulting in underachievement. If, however, diagnostic tests are used they should *not* be regarded as a substitute for other forms of information gathering. As stated above, information should influence the framing of teaching/learning strategies on a continual basis and not just periodically.

3)    Personalised or informal diagnostic tests.

The tutor's own form of diagnostic assessment is preferable to giving the student a whole battery of formal tests. The advantages of this are that the content of the test is controlled by the tutor, and that it is directly related to the needs of the individual student. As with published tests, these individualised diagnostic tests should only be used to supplement the information obtained by careful observation in the ordinary teaching situation.

● **Analysis**

Once information has been gathered, either by observation or testing, it needs to be analysed before it can be acted on. Discussion with the student is again of particular importance as he can supply his own perceptions of what his performance was and what his future needs are. Analysis of mistakes is essential with any set work. The tutor is there to promote learning, learning does not take place simply by marking 'sums' right or wrong! Instead he needs to examine the work carefully and decide upon the nature of the errors so that he can help the student to avoid them in the future.

This is usually a straightforward business but there is always the danger that a wrong interpretation will be made especially when only one example is being analysed. For instance, if a student is presented with 6 X 2 and arrives at the answer 8, without having further information any of the following interpretations is possible: a) that the student thinks the sign 'X' is an instruction to add, b) that he simply misread 'X' for '+', c) that he made a mistake in terms of accuracy, ie that he thinks 6 X 2 is 8, or, d) that the answer is a guess. Of course, this danger can usually be avoided by presenting more than one example. (Personalised diagnostic tests should normally have 3 or 4 examples of each sub-skill being assessed in order to supply sufficient information for analysis.)

In any analysis it is important to differentiate between a mistaken or misunderstood concept, and an innacuracy made when calculating. Different teaching approaches will be needed for each case. For instance, the types of error displayed by student A are very different from those of B.

| | | |
|---|---|---|
| (A) | 53 | 48 |
| | X  7 | X  4 |
| | 1210 | 812 |
| (B) | 53 | 48 |
| | X  7 | X  4 |
| | 301 | 190 |

Clearly, (A) has no concept of either multiplication nor place value and is simply adding up the digits, while (B), although arriving at inaccurate answers, at least understands the processes involved. In terms of future teaching (B) should be directed to either use a multiplication square or multiplication tables until he has mastered greater accuracy, whereas (A) needs to be introduced both to the fundamentals of multiplication and the concept of place value.

## 1.6 The importance of recording progress

Some form of monitoring and recording progress is essential. A record of work is useful not only to yourself, but also to scheme organisers, and, where appropriate, class tutors. Furthermore, a student has the right to know how he is getting on, and some form of written record is an indication of the amount of work he has covered.

Records can be kept in a variety of ways, though where tutors need to consult with each other it may be more efficient to adopt a similar format. There is little purpose served by writing up highly detailed reports on each lesson. As with diagnosis, the writing of records is not an end in itself: the purpose should dictate their form. Most tutors will need little more than brief notes to indicate what has been taught, problems encountered, and suggestions for future activities. Obviously, if these are to be used by other tutors they must avoid being so cryptic that little information can be gleaned.

Possible forms of notation are either the record sheet as suggested under 'Diagnosis'(p.12) or one which is basically a check-list of sub-skills, such as:

| Concept/Operation | Problems encountered | Date |
|---|---|---|
| Concept of number | none | 9/9 |
| Recognition of written numbers | reverses digits | 9/9 |
| Addition (to 10) | needs written practice | 16/9 |
| Subtraction (to 10) | | |
| Addition (to 20) | none | 23/9 |
| Subtraction (to 20) | | |

14

However, such check-lists may need to be supplemented by further notes, and most importantly the sequence they outline should not be adopted rigidly. Thus, in the example given, tutor and student have proceeded to addition of numbers up to 20 before introducing subtraction.

## 1.7 Resources for learning

There is already a great deal of equipment and text books designed to help develop an understanding of basic mathematical concepts and increase fluency in their manipulations, but these are on the whole designed for school children. Most published texts, while no doubt suitable for their particular purposes, are inappropriate for use with adults. The illustrations they contain are embarrassingly childlike in content and though few students may overtly object to them, they help reinforce a self-perception which is unproductive. Moreover, because of their rigid adherence to a particular sequential structure many are inappropriate for use in individual and small group work typical of adult numeracy. Perhaps, most seriously, they are of little use with adults because the examples they refer to are drawn from the world of children; they are concerned in the main not with calculating wages or household budgeting, but with marbles and conkers!

It may not be a bad thing that we have little published material to draw on. It makes us as tutors fall back on the resources which students themselves use: shopping lists, timetables, costings, bills, etc. and in doing so this inevitably brings the student into a more central role in formulating his own learning programme.

Home-made materials can be produced inexpensively and in very little time. The use of items such as travel brochures, adverts from newspapers and magazines cost nothing, and yet present numerous occasions for calculations involving number. Worksheets relating to them can easily be devised and the units, if stored, either in terms of mathematical skills or themes (or cross-referenced) can form the basis of a steadily growing resources centre. Schools, because they cater for large numbers of students, have to use commercially produced equipment — counters, plastic fractions, etc. Although some apparatus can be of value when teaching adults, everyday objects — pens, paperclips, and paper will be far more useful and acceptable.

However, on occasions it may be useful to have books, or duplicated sheets, containing written calculations so that the student can increase his fluency by practice. Having these in printed form will save the tutors a considerable amount of time and, wherever possible the answers should be accessible to students. Such practice work is only one part of the total numeracy programme and should not take up too much time as it can become exceedingly boring. However, in small doses it can reinforce the knowledge of the particular sub-skills introduced earlier in the lesson.

Useful books for students:

*Make it Count Student Workbook,* Laxton, R. and Rawlinson, G., National Extension College, 1977.
*Make it Count Puzzles,* Chester, J. and Avis, P., National Extension College, 1977.

Hesse, K. A. *Four Rules of Number,* Longmans, 1956. Books of practice examples which are finely graded. Answer books also available.
Moore, N. and Williams, A. *Mathematics for Life,* O.U.P., 1976. Designed to prepare older secondary pupils for everyday mathematical situations. Adopts a broad approach with ideas that can easily be adapted for use with adults. However, many of the actual examples and illustrations used in the texts are obviously geared to the interests of adolescents.

A *Make it Count card game* by Chris Woodhouse, is also published by the National Extension College.

# PART II   THE NATURE AND SEQUENCING OF NUMBER SUBSKILLS

## Introduction

The approach to numeracy tuition advocated in this manual is one in which the basic skills whenever possible are taught through real life situations. However, if the teaching is to be effective it is important that the work is structured. The basic number skills need to be introduced in sequence and each stage consolidated before progressing to the next.

Learning will be more effective not only if the skills are practised in a context which is directly relevant to the student, but also if the student understands what he is doing and why he is doing it. It is of course possible to learn by rote, but there are four major drawbacks in using this method with adults.

● In most cases it will have been the approach adopted when the student was at school and has already failed him.

● It relies solely on one ability — the ability to remember — which may in any case be declining with increasing age. If other cognitive abilities are employed the chances that learning will effectively take place will be increased.

● Rote learning can never ensure that the student can transfer a real problem he is presented with into the appropriate written calculation.

● If a student does not understand the processes involved the possibility of error is increased.

Thus there is a need for a programme of work which while related to the student's everyday needs, must be structured in such a way that he can easily progress, as his understanding develops, through clearly defined and finely graded stages. However, any structure or sequence is essentially no more than an aid. It is only too easy to begin to think that it has some value in itself and to rigidly adhere to it, when with a little imagination and flexibility a more effective learning programme could be devised.

The sequence outlined here may not always correspond to what a student already knows. For instance, you may find that the student is familiar with graphs and averages (introduced in the final section of Part II) and yet have difficulty with, say, long multiplication. The order in which we have introduced the sub-skills does not have to be rigidly followed. It is more in the nature of a check-list of sub-skills which a student needs to acquire, with simple teaching tips where appropriate. *At all times the needs of the student are of paramount importance, and as a tutor you must fulfil such needs rather than mechanically work through this or any other programme of numeracy teaching.* You may also find that your student wishes, because of the nature of his job, to know more about particular topics (eg fractions) or to be familiar with processes not mentioned here (eg conversion of imperial measurements into metric units) and so you may need to include additional work not covered here. What we are providing is a common denominator of the basic number work all adults need. Individual requirements may necessitate going into far greater detail about particular operations and concepts.

The rest of part II is devoted to the detailed elaboration of one numeracy teaching programme, and uses the same order sequence of skills as the *Make it Count* student workbook.

The teaching programme has two basic features:

● It stresses the interrelationships between the four number operations or 'rules'

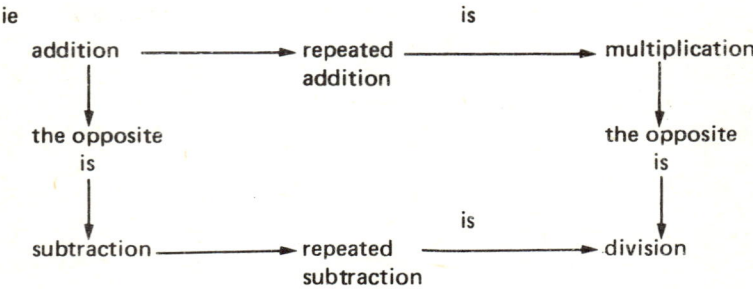

● The work is graded by the size of numbers and not the operations involved. Thus sections 1—3 deal with addition, subtraction, multiplication and division of numbers up to 20, sections 4—6 all operations on numbers to 100, and so on.

## Section 2.1 Numbers up to 10

### 2.1.1 Understanding numbers and basic mental addition
If a student is at a very basic stage in number work it is first important to establish whether he has a consistent understanding of number, eg can he repeatedly recognise the quantity 6 for what it is?

Present the student with a number of mixed objects, eg pens, pencils, paper clips. At this initial stage, keep these quantities below 10. Ask how many there are of each. If the student responds accurately, see if he can add two of these groups together. If not, proceed to more concrete work of this type, simply building up the concept of numbers from 1 to 10.

## 2.1.2 Recognition of numbers

The student should learn at the same time to recognise a written number. So, having asked him to identify the number of objects, he then writes down that number. Again, this activity would initially be restricted to 1 to 10.

To make sure the student does recognise numbers, invent simple recognition games:

eg Join up by lines and arrows numbers that are the same.

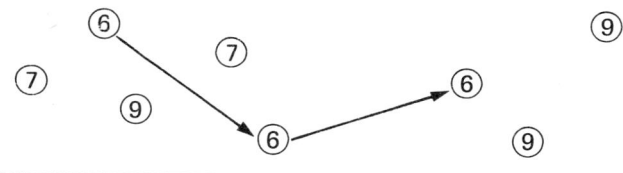

Cover up numbers on cards, as in bingo. In this game, the number of figures used will depend upon the ability of the student. It can either be played by a group of students of similar ability, or by a tutor calling the number and a student/students covering the numbers.

| | 6 | 5 |
|---|---|---|
| 9 | | |

| 3 | | |
|---|---|---|
| | 6 | 5 |

| 5 | | 6 |
|---|---|---|
| | 2 | |

### 2.1.3 Number sequence

It is very important that a student realises that there is a set pattern in which numbers occur.

For numbers 1 to 10, this sequence can best be demonstrated by means of a number line. This can be simply drawn on a piece of paper, or constructed in the form of a tape measure.

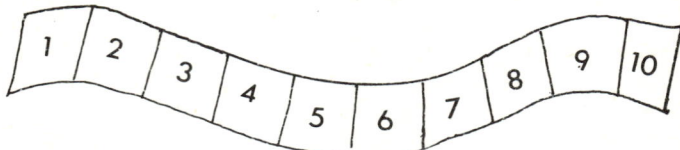

Begin by asking a student to count *on* from a given point. Then proceed to counting *backwards*.

Again, simple games can be used. The student is presented with a group of numbers.

These can be used in various ways. Eg by means of lines and arrows, show the numbers in sequence, starting from the lowest *or* starting from the highest going down in sequence, *or* starting at a mid-point, and going up or down.

### 2.1.4 Addition of numbers below 10

Once it has been established that the student has a thorough understanding of the previous concepts, the next stage is to introduce simple addition. If the student has difficulty in dealing with numbers in the abstract, use either concrete apparatus, eg counters or coins, or the number line mentioned above.

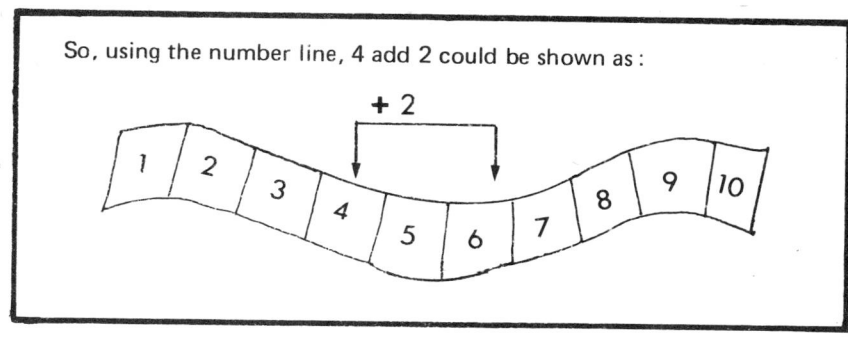

So, using the number line, 4 add 2 could be shown as :

**+ 2**

After working with the number line, a student could be introduced to formally written sums. Although he may rarely see numbers presented as such in everyday life, he may need this skill in his job, or indeed in connection with simple problems around the home.

Explain that an addition sum can be presented in a number of different ways, eg

3 + 6 = ☐          3 +          3
                      6          + 6
                     ───         ───

                     ───         ───

You will need to explain the meaning of the addition sign, and that it can occur in a variety of places. You may also need to explain that addition sums can be written either horizontally or vertically, yet both methods give the same answer.

## Section 2.2 The importance of 10

In section 2.1, we dealt with the recognition and addition of numbers up to ten. In the second section, we are emphasising the importance of ten itself in our number system.

21

## 2.2.1 Number bonds

To emphasise the importance of 10 it is necessary to examine its construction. The term 'number bond' is used to cover the individual numbers which a larger number can be broken down into, eg: the number bonds of 7 are 2 and 5, 1 and 6, and 3 and 4. The aim of teaching number bonds is to demonstrate to the student that a number can be built up in various ways.

Present the student with a number of addition sums, in which the answer is always 10. Such as

$$4 + 6 = \square \qquad 5 + 2 + 3 = \square \qquad \begin{array}{r} 7 \\ 2 \\ + 1 \\ \hline \\ \hline \end{array} \qquad \begin{array}{r} 9 \\ + 1 \\ \hline \\ \hline \end{array}$$

This can also be presented in another form

ie

$$3 + \square = 10 \qquad 8 + \square = 10 \qquad \square + 6 = 10$$

This form will involve the student in the process of 'adding on' — that is, he starts with a number, eg 3, and 'adds on' until he comes to 10. This process of addition can be very useful, especially if a student is involved in dealing with money, since it is a method commonly used in giving change.

Because 10 is very important in our number system, the student should practise addition up to this number until he can add up rapidly both in mental and written form.

## 2.2.2 Numbers 10—19

Having established the significance of 10, it can be shown that the numbers 10—19 are formed by simply adding a single digit to this base of 10.

It may be useful at this stage for a student to begin to construct a 100 square, filling in numbers as they are introduced :

| 1 | 2 | 3 | 4 | 5 | 6 | 7 | 8 | 9 | 10 |
|---|---|---|---|---|---|---|---|---|----|
| 11 | 12 | 13 | 14 | 15 | 16 | 17 | 18 | 19 | |

It is very important to emphasise that the numbers 11—19 are made up of tens and ones.

ie

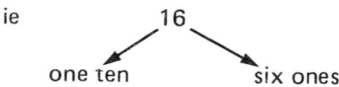

one ten          six ones

*It is essential to establish a thorough understanding of place value because it is the basis for all future mathematical work.*

To see if the student has understood this, present him with a selection of numbers from 1—19.

9

19                    11                    17

10

Ask questions such as:

which number has nine ones?

which number has no tens?

which number has one ten and one one?

which number has no ones?

### 2.2.3 Concept of 20

So far, it has been demonstrated to the student that the basis of our number system is 10. Having explained the principle of building upon this with single digits for numbers 11-19, we then introduce 20.

It is important to emphasise that 20 consists of two tens and no ones.

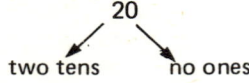

two tens      no ones

10 + 10 = 20

This can also be a useful way of introducing the first principles of multiplication, explained as:

two *lots of ten* = 20

*or*    2 X 10 = 20

## 2.2.4 Addition up to 20

Present the student with a sum such as:

```
   8
+  2
____
```

Since the student has already met vertical addition in section 2.1, he will know how to begin this sum, either mentally or with concrete objects.

```
tens  ones
        8
+       2
 1      0
```

Having arrived at the answer, however, he will need an explanation where to place the digits. At this early stage this may be best explained by placing the word 'ones' above the existing numbers, and the word 'tens' above what will be the new column.

Exactly the same process should be repeated for a sum such as:

```
tens  ones
        9
+       3
 1      2
```

The only difference here of course is that the answer, 12, consists of both tens and ones. Discuss with the student how many ones and how many tens the answer contains, and write the answer accordingly.

24

The next stage in the addition process is the introduction of digits in the tens column.

| tens | ones | |
|------|------|---|
| 1 | 6 | If the student is writing the sum out himself, make |
| + | 3 | sure that the digits are placed in the correct column. |
| 1 | 9 | Go on to explain that initially he approaches this |

If the student is writing the sum out himself, make sure that the digits are placed in the correct column. Go on to explain that initially he approaches this problem in exactly the same way as the one above, ie start by adding the ones. Having done that, then go on to the tens column.

When you have worked through section 2.2.4 it will be obvious how important a real understanding of place value is. Without this, the above section becomes a series of rules which the student may, or may not, follow correctly. You should bear in mind that the reason for your student's original failure in mathematics may be that he was taught simply by rote, without any attempt made at explaining basic principles. Therefore, although a student may need a lot of practice to establish the process of addition, he must also have a thorough understanding of the concept.

## Section 2.3 The relationship between the four mathematical operations

When teaching mathematical ideas, it is very important that each rule is not taught in isolation, but rather a relationship is built up between the principles involved. In this section an attempt is made to show how the four operations of number work can be taught side-by-side.

### 2.3.1 Introducing subtraction

So that the student can have a good grounding in what subtraction means, it must be shown that basically it is the reversal of addition.

To demonstrate this, it may be easiest to go back to the number line suggested in section 2.1.3.

As with the process of addition, begin with numbers below 10. We have already seen that the line can be used to show $2 + 6 = 8$

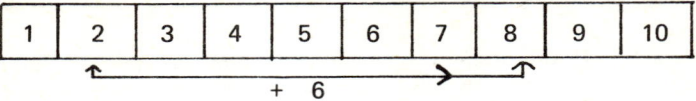

We can now use the line to show the reverse of this $8 - 6 = 2$

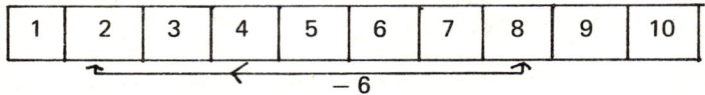

When the student understands this, extend the line to 20, or beyond if required.

To build up the idea of the relationship between addition and subtraction, simple exercises can be devised.

Below are three examples using the same numbers:

    a) $6 - 2 = \square$
    b) $6 - \square = 4$
    c) $\square - 2 = 4$

a) is a straightforward example of subtraction in which 2 is simply taken away from 6. In example b) however, the sum is easiest tackled in the way of an addition sum — ie starting at 4, 'count on' until arriving at 6. The number counted on goes into the box. The addition method is also applied to example c), where we *add* the 2 and 4 together to get the original number.

## 2.3.2 Vertical subtraction.

You can show the student that simple vertical subtraction is tackled in exactly the same way as when it is laid out horizontally.

Use a number of examples:

9 − 4 = 5 is the same as

$$\begin{array}{r} 9 \\ -\ 4 \\ \hline 5 \\ \hline \end{array}$$

or

$$\begin{array}{r} 9- \\ 4 \\ \hline 5 \\ \hline \end{array}$$

Make sure that the student writes the answer in the correct position, ie in the ones column, straight underneath his line of work.

It is worth pointing out, even at this very early stage that calculations involving subtraction can be checked by reversing the process to one of addition. Thus in the example here 9 − 4 = 5, the student should be encouraged to double check ie 4 + 5 = 9. Double checking should not be done with every calculation because this will result in a habit developing which will ultimately slow the student down in situations where speed is important.

The next stage is the introduction of a tens column.

As with addition, this type of sum can be put into two labelled columns, tens and ones, if this makes it clearer for the student. eg

$$\begin{array}{cc} \text{tens} & \text{ones} \\ 1 & 5 \\ - & 3 \\ \hline \\ \hline \end{array}$$

## 2.3.3 Multiplication

As we stated in the introduction to part II it is important to stress to a student the relationship between each of the number 'rules'. This relationship can be seen very clearly between multiplication and addition, since multiplication is simply the repeated addition of the same number. Because of the connection between the two processes, the easiest way of introducing multiplication is by addition.

Present the student with some practical situation, such as:

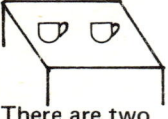 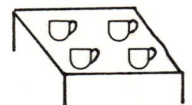

There are two cups on a table

Another two are added

As an addition sum this would be;

2 + 2 = 4

Another way of putting this is that;

two *lots of* two = 4

*or* 2 X 2 = 4

Another two cups are added, so;

2 + 2 + 2 = 6

*or* three *lots of* two = 6

*or* 3 X 2 = 6

By explaining that there are three *lots of* two we emphasise the idea of groups of numbers. Once the student has understood this, then it can be explained that saying *3 times 2* is simply a shorthand version of this.

Some students may find the concept of multiplication difficult. If this is the case, concrete materials should be used eg if one wanted to demonstrate counting in two's make repeated groups of the same objects, eg 1p coins.

2 + 2 + 2 + 2 = 8

*or* four *lots of* two = 8

*or* 4 X 2 = 8

Having established the idea that multiplication is simply recurrent addition, you can use this idea to introduce a student to multiplication tables:

Using objects if necessary, you can show that:

| | | |
|---|---|---|
| 2+2 = 4 | is the same as | 2 X 2 = 4 |
| 2+2+2 = 6 | is the same as | 3 X 2 = 6 |
| 2+2+2+2 = 8 | is the same as | 4 X 2 = 8 |
| 2+2+2+2+2 = 10 | is the same as | 5 X 2 = 10 |
| 2+2+2+2+2+2 = 12 | is the same as | 6 X 2 = 12 |
| 2+2+2+2+2+2+2 = 14 | is the same as | 7 X 2 = 14 |
| 2+2+2+2+2+2+2+2 = 16 | is the same as | 8 X 2 = 16 |
| 2+2+2+2+2+2+2+2+2 = 18 | is the same as | 9 X 2 = 18 |
| 2+2+2+2+2+2+2+2+2+2 = 20 | is the same as | 10 X 2 = 20 |

Exactly the same process can be done for other multiplication tables. To simplify matters for the student, initially restrict this work to answers up to 20.

At this stage you may find it helpful to work with your student in constructing a multiplication square.

| 1 | 2 | 3 | 4 | 5 | 6 | 7 | 8 | 9 | 10 | 11 | 12 |
|---|---|---|---|---|---|---|---|---|---|---|---|
| 2 | 4 | 6 | 8 | 10 | 12 | 14 | 16 | 18 | 20 | | |
| 3 | 6 | 9 | 12 | 15 | 18 | | | | | | |
| 4 | 8 | 12 | 16 | 20 | | | | | | | |
| 5 | 10 | 15 | 20 | | | | | | | | |
| 6 | 12 | 18 | | | | | | | | | |
| 7 | 14 | | | | | | | | | | |
| 8 | 16 | | | | | | | | | | |
| 9 | 18 | | | | | | | | | | |
| 10 | 20 | | | | | | | | | | |
| 11 | | | | | | | | | | | |
| 12 | | | | | | | | | | | |

The square can be used in a variety of ways:

- If the student wishes to learn a particular table, then it can either be written out for him, or he can construct it himself.
- If a student is not able to remember a table, then he can be shown how to use the square to find an answer.
- It is very easy to show the reversability of tables on the square, ie 3 X 2 = 6, is the same as 2 X 3 = 6

### 2.3.4 Vertical multiplication

In section 2.3.3 above we explained the connection between horizontal multiplication and repeated addition. You can now show that vertical and horizontal multiplication give the same results.

so
```
   2      is the same as    4 X 2 = 8
   2
   2
 + 2      and as            4
   8                      X 2
                            8
```

or
```
   3      is the same as    3 X 3 = 9
   3
 + 3                        3
   9      and as          X 3
                            9
```

The next stage is to introduce calculations with answers larger than 9.

```
eg    6     Make sure the student places the ten in the correct
    X 2     column. Again, if the concept of ten has been fully
     12     understood, there should be no problems with place
            value.
```

### 2.3.5 Division

Multiplication has been explained as a process which involved the repeated addition of a number. Similarly, you should explain division, as a process of repeated subtraction. However, it may be easier for the student to understand what is involved in division if he is taught that it is a means of breaking up a number into smaller, equal groups. Initially this could be demonstrated by sharing a number of identical objects between a group of people.

At the same time as explaining the process of division, introduce simple division sums.

Using the example of 12 objects to be divided between three people, first discuss the principle and then demonstrate in practical terms.

Explain to the student that as a written sum, this problem could appear as:

$$12 \div 3 = \square \quad \text{or} \quad 3 \underline{)12} \quad \text{or} \quad 3 \overline{)12}$$

the latter being the most common.

In order to show the relationship between multiplication and division, it may be useful to reverse the above sum so that $12 \div 3 = 4$ is shown to be the opposite of $3 \times 4 = 12$.

As with multiplication, the student can be shown how to arrive at the answer through using the multiplication square or tables.

## Section 2.4  Developing the four operations

### 2.4.1  Numbers 20-29

In section 2.2.3 we introduced the idea of 20 as the product of two tens. From that stage the student can be shown how to build upon the number 20, to form the numbers 21-29.

Referring back to section 2.2.3, the same stages of development can be followed.

1)  Make sure that the student understands the composition of numbers 20-29, in terms of tens and ones, eg

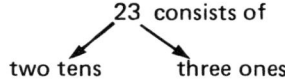

23 consists of

two tens          three ones

Perhaps this can be more easily demonstrated in terms of money. Given a pile of 10p and 1p pieces, see if the student can build up

31

appropriate sums of money

eg

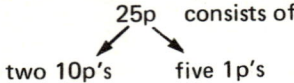

25p    consists of

two 10p's        five 1p's

*Note:* Once the student is competent in working with 20, the same method can be used for any multiple of 10 up to 100.

2) Continue with the 100 number square, filling in the numbers 20—29. Again, use this to show how numbers are built up, and how they form a definite pattern.

3) Devise simple sums and exercises to reinforce the above points:

    eg  a) Ask the student to change twenty-seven 1p pieces into units of 10's and 1's.

        b) ◯ + ◯ +⑩+⑩+⑩+⑩+⑩+⑩+⑩+⑩= 29p

            ?      ?

        What are the missing coins?

    c)                 29         2

      26                        23

        19          12

What are the missing coins?

    Which numbers have two ones?

    Which number has two tens and nine ones?

    How many numbers have two tens?

## 2.4.2 Addition, with carrying

The student has already been introduced to the idea of vertical addition. So far though, this has been restricted to single digits, or the presence of one ten only. Next the student is introduced to addition of tens as well as ones.

At first, the student should be introduced to two figure addition, where *no* carrying is involved.

eg .  2  3      Make sure that the student reads the answer as one
   +  1  4      number, ie in this example, 37, rather than a 3 and
   ─────        a 7.
      3  7

Present your student with an example,

eg    2  6      Make sure he begins with the ones column.
   +  3  8      As the number 14 is greater than 9, he must split it
   ─────        up into a ten and ones. The ones he can put into
      6  4      the ones column, but the one ten must go into the
   ─────        tens column.
      1          N.B. At this stage you may wish to point out that
                the one ten can go either *above* or *below*, the answer
                is either;

(a)   2  6      or      (b)   2  6
   +3 1 8                  +  3  8
   ──────                  ──────
         4                       4
   ──────                  ──────
                                 1

In *Make it Count* the method as shown in example (a) has been
chosen. In this manual, example (b) has been followed. Whichever
method is chosen, make sure that the student realises that the 1
stands for one ten and must be added to the other tens.
The student now completes the sum by adding up the tens.

## 2.4.3 Simple subtraction of numbers less than 100

The student now proceeds to subtraction of numbers between 20 and 100,
although as yet without employing decomposition.

You should show the student an example,

eg    8  4      Point out that the only difference between this and
   −  5  2      earlier subtraction sums is that the subtraction
   ─────        process now applies also to the tens column.
   ─────

## 2.4.4 Multiples of 10 up to 100

So far it has been pointed out that our number system is based on 10. The student is now introduced to multiples of 10 up to 100.

You can build up a progressive chart as shown in Part 4 of *Make it Count*, demonstrating these multiples from 10 to 90, ie

$$20 = 10 + 10$$

$$30 = 10 + 10 + 10$$

$$40 = 10 + 10 + 10 + 10 \text{ etc.}$$

Since a lot of our number work is done in tens, try to ensure that your student can deal quickly with these numbers. Some suggestions of how this can be done are:

• Ask a student to count up and down in tens, starting from either 10 or 100  or choose a number, eg 40 or 50, and ask a student to go up or down from there.

• Present the student with horizontal sums in which he has to fill in the blank, eg

60 + □    = 80

□  +   10  = 40

50 +   20  = □

• Use the example of money and ask questions such as;

How many 10p's are there in 60p?

How much change would you get from 50p if you spend 30p?

• If a student drives, he will be familiar with road signs in units of 10. These can be used in simple addition sums, eg

  A man is going at 30 mph. If he was going 20 mph faster how fast would he be going?

  What is the difference in speed between these two signs?

To test the student's understanding of place value, use the exercise introduced previously, of presenting a random selection of numbers.

49
80          63          52
56                      96
          37
          50

The student can then be asked,

- To join up all the numbers which have 5 tens.
- Which numbers are above 50?
- Starting with the lowest, join up the numbers in order of size.
- Which number is the answer to 30 + 50?
- Which number is 10 less than 60?

## 2.4.5 Multiplication by 10

In Section 2.3.3 it was shown that multiplication is simply a speedy method of repeated addition. This was demonstrated by means of the two times table. Now we have shown in 2.4.4 above the composition of multiples of ten, these can be related to the ten times table.

You can show the student that,

$$10+10 = 20 \quad \text{is the same as} \quad 2 \times 10 = 20$$
$$10+10+10 = 30 \quad \text{is the same as} \quad 3 \times 10 = 30$$
$$10+10+10+10 = 40 \quad \text{is the same as} \quad 4 \times 10 = 40$$

and so on.

After building up the ten times table, the student may be able to recognise for himself the simple method of multiplying by 10, ie the addition of a nought to the original number.
Give your student a good deal of practice writing down answers to questions such as 6 X 10 = □ , 62 X 10 = □ , but also ask him to *read* out the answer, for this, of course, is the difficult part. Having moved each number one place to the left by the addition of the nought, the place value of each digit has been altered. This is in fact a good method of finding out how much a student has understood about how the value of numbers depend on their position and relationship to each other.

## Section 2.5 More on multiplication and division

### 2.5.1 Other multiplication tables

So far, the student has been introduced to the two and ten times tables only, although mention has been made of multiplication by other figures. As the student progresses, you should introduce other tables, remembering that these should be first taught as repeated addition. *The order in which the multiplication tables are taught is very important.* They should not be introduced as a simple progression, starting at 2 and working upwards, but rather a relationship between multiples should be established.

---

After teaching the two times table, the relationship between that and the four times table can be shown.

| | | |
|---|---|---|
| 2 X 2 = 4 | or | 1 X 4 = 4 |
| 4 X 2 = 8 | | 2 X 4 = 8 |
| 6 X 2 = 12 | | 3 X 4 = 12 |

Thus since 4 is the product of two 2's, then the product of each of the equivalent multiples shows the same property.

This group of tables would also include the eight times table.

Again, after teaching the ten times table, a connection should be made between this and the five times table. Similarly you should point out the relationship between the multiples of 3, 6, and 9. The twelve times table could also be included here.

The seven times table, and the eleven times, if you wish to go beyond ten, can only be taught by themselves, since 7 and 11 are prime numbers.

---

Undoubtedly, in many situations the ability to multiply simple numbers quickly is essential. You may find, however, that your student has great difficulty in remembering multiples. If this is the case, do not labour the point but simply show your student how to work from a multiplication square. Remember, that for many students learning multiplication tables by rote conjures up painful memories of their schooldays. Eventually, through continual reference to the multiplication square, a working knowledge of the multiples will be gained.

### 2.5.2 Multiplication with tens and ones

Now we have dealt with the multiplication of one-digit numbers, a tens figure is introduced.

36

```
eg    1 4        If the student does not know the two times tables,
   X    2        use either the table as written down, or the student's
      2 8        multiplication square.
```
If the student does not know the two times tables, use either the table as written down, or the student's multiplication square.

Make sure that the student knows that he begins by multiplying the ones, before proceeding to the tens.

Occasionally it may be advisable for the student to check his own work by converting the multiplication sum into one using addition.

## 2.5.3 Multiplication with carrying

Once the student has had practice in simple multiplication, and can successfully apply the multiplication tables, the next stage is to introduce carrying from the ones to the tens column.

Since the student has already become acquainted with the carrying of tens during addition (Section 2.4.2) the idea will not be totally new to him. Despite this, you will still need to show him how it applies in multiplication. Give the student an example,

```
  2 5        
X   3        
  7 5        
  1          
```

First, ask the student which multiplication table he must use, and then ask him to find the answer for the ones column of 5 X 3. Having found the product 15, the student breaks this down into tens and ones.

NB  As with addition, the ten can be placed either above or below the answer space, as long as it is clearly in the tens column. As a student gets more proficient, of course, he may feel he does not need to write this figure down at all, and can simply remember it.

He then proceeds to multiply the tens figure (2 X 3 = 6) and adds on the 1 ten he carried, making a total of 7 tens.

## 2.5.4 Division, with remainders

The idea of division as an equal sharing out of parts has already been discussed (Section 2.3.5). The student needs also to be aware of the fact that frequently there is a remainder.

This is best illustrated at first in practical terms. Keep the example simple, and present it in ways which the student will understand, possibly using real objects, eg pens or coins, and initially restricting it to division by 2. After division by 2, more complicated examples can be introduced

eg   $16 \div 5$

Again, using a practical example to illustrate this, it can be explained as 16 objects have to be divided between 5 people.

• 1 object
  left over.

ie      $16 \div 5 = 3$, with one left over

or      $5 \overline{)16}^{\,3}$   with 1 left over

In this early stage, where the student may be using practical apparatus to share out the units, it is relatively easy. The difficulty appears when the student attempts this without practical help. Taking as an example $5 \overline{)16}$   the student can be shown how to use his multiplication square as an aid. By referring him to the 5 in the outside vertical column, he can follow this line horizontally along until he comes to the figure just below the number he is dividing. In this case he would arrive at the number 15. He then goes vertically up the column, and arrives at his answer, 3.

15 is 1 less than 16, so the answer to   $5 \overline{)16}$ is 3, with 1 left over.

In Part 5 of *Make it Count*, it is shown how a student can use a multiplication table to find the same answer. Either method, however, can be very complicated for a student, and does rely on him being able to recognise the number just below the figure he is searching for, ie in our example that 15 is just below 16, the figure given. It is therefore important both to explain clearly what the process involves and how to carry it out accurately.

## Section 2.6 Methods of subtraction

### 2.6.1 Subtraction using decomposition

So far, the work done using subtraction has been restricted to examples where the top figure in the ones column is greater than the number to be subtracted from it.

The next stage is to introduce a figure in the ones column which is greater than the number it is to be subtracted from.

The method adopted here and in *Make it Count* is decomposition.

---

Let us take as an example the sum

$$\begin{array}{r} 6\ 3 \\ -\ 2\ 5 \\ \hline \end{array}$$

When the student is given a sum such as this he will, as always, begin with the ones column,

$$\begin{array}{r} 3 \\ -\ 5 \\ \hline \end{array}$$

He is immediately faced with the problem that he cannot take 5 from 3, and has to learn a new technique to cope with this. The advantage of the decomposition method of subtraction is that, if necessary, it can be easily demonstrated by means of apparatus.

At this initial stage it may be advisable to either use different coloured counters to represent tens and ones, or better still, to use 10p and 1p coins. Thus the top line in our example would be set out as:

tens        ones

⑩ ⑩      ① ①
⑩ ⑩      ①
⑩ ⑩

Since 5 cannot be subtracted from 3, we have to make the number of ones greater in the top line by *decomposing* 1 ten. The student will know from previous work that 1 ten is composed of 10 ones. Therefore, he should be quite ready to accept the fact that we can take 1 ten and change it into 10 ones, so making a total of 13 ones in the top line.

It may help if the student actually changes one 10p coin into ten 1p's. This procedure is written in the sum as;

```
tens   ones
 ⁵6̸     ¹3
-2      5
```

or, with the coins as;

```
tens   ones
⑩ ⑩   ①p ①p
⑩ ⑩   ①p ①p
⑩     ①p ①p
      ①p ①p
      ①p ①p
      ①p ①p
      ①p
```

He can now proceed with the subtraction. The ones column now reads;

```
  13
-  5
─────
   8
─────
```

The student then goes on to the tens column. Since we had to transfer one of these tens, this column now reads as;

```
   5
-  2
─────
   3
─────
```

The whole sum, therefore, reads like this, when completed

```
tens   ones
 ⁵6̸     ¹3
-2      5
─────────
 3      8
─────────
```

## 2.6.2 Subtraction using equal addition

Although subtraction using decomposition is both more straightforward and easier to demonstrate, and thus should be taught to students being introduced to subtraction, some will have been taught, and half remember, the equal addition method. It is important that the student should not be confused by introducing a different method. As a tutor you need to discuss this matter with your student, find out which method he uses, and adapt your approach accordingly.

You should explain to the student that subtraction by equal addition is based on the fact that 10 is added to the top and the bottom line in order to facilitate the calculation. However, the ten added to the top line is in the form of 10 ones, whereas on the bottom line it takes the form of 1 ten. Thus, using the previous example it would be written as

$$
\begin{array}{r}
6\ {}^{1}3 \\
2_{1}\,5 \\
\hline
3\ 8 \\
\hline
\end{array}
$$

the ones column looks exactly the same as the decomposition method.

$$
\begin{array}{r}
1\ 3 \\
-\ \ \ 5 \\
\hline
8 \\
\hline
\end{array}
$$

The tens column looks different because instead of subtracting the ten from the top line, we have added it to the bottom line, so it now reads

$$
\begin{array}{r}
6 \\
-\ 3 \\
\hline
3 \\
\hline
\end{array}
$$

The whole sum looks like this,

$$
\begin{array}{r}
6\ {}^{1}3 \\
-\ 2_{1}\,5 \\
\hline
3\ 8 \\
\hline
\end{array}
$$

But the answer is the same!

## Section 2.7 More advanced processes: estimating, larger numbers and fractions

### 2.7.1 Estimating

An important aspect of numeracy in everyday adult life is the ability to estimate.

Although estimating implies an approximate answer, it cannot be described as guess work. For behind the ability to estimate reasonably accurately there lies a good grounding in the different skills of basic numeracy.

A student can be introduced to the idea of estimating through basic number work.

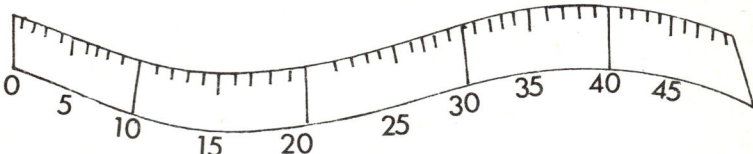

Using a number line, begin with the numbers 10—20. Explain that the mid-point between these two numbers is 15. Numbers below 15 are nearer to 10, numbers above, nearer to 20.
You can use a tape measure or devise your own number line. Give the student various numbers between these two points, and ask him which number, 10 or 20, they are nearest to. Once the idea has been established, the method can be expanded.

eg    Is 37 nearer to 30 or 40?
      Which multiple of 10 is nearest to 83?

Thus the student develops the ability to round off numbers to the nearest 10. He can then proceed to adding two numbers together.
Let us take for example the sum    24
                                  + 31
                                  ‾‾‾‾

First take the number 24.
Ask the student which multiple of 10 is nearest to 24.
Then ask the same for the 31.
Since the student has previously learnt how to count in 10's, he should be able to add these two figures together and arrive at the approximate answer 50.
In order to be completely accurate, the student can then do the sum in the usual way, beginning with the ones, and then progressing to the tens.

The ability to estimate proves very useful in checking the answer to a sum, or, alternatively, in giving a rough guide beforehand as to what the final answer will be.

You should also estimate when you are subtracting. In the example
of   58
  − 27
  ‾‾‾‾

  ‾‾‾‾

the student again rounds off the numbers to the nearest 10.

It should then be relatively easy for him to subtract 30 from 60. As a result, he will find out the *approximate* answer to the sum. Again, in order to find the exact answer, he can do the sum in the normal way, using the approximation as a guide.

The benefits of being able to estimate are many. When you have dealt with the basis of estimating, as above, try presenting the student with everyday situations in which these principles can be applied, eg in relation to money.

Examples could be:

● A box of chocolates is reduced to 49p. Approximately how much would 4 boxes cost?

● A bill is made up of the following prices.

47p
12p          What is the approximate cost of the goods?
51p
16p
‾‾‾‾

‾‾‾‾

● From a total of £1, is it possible to spend 48p on cigarettes, 19p on a cup of coffee, and 12p on a bus fare?

In all these problems the student rounds off the figures to the nearest 10p. He then proceeds to do a calculation involving either addition or subtraction, in order to find the approximate answer.

## 2.7.2 Place value of numbers in the hundreds

Up till now we have dealt only with numbers up to 99. In this section the student is introduced to numbers beyond 100. The relationship between 10 and 100 should be explained.

10+10+10+10+10+10+10+10+10+10 = 100

    10 *lots of* 10    = 100

    10 X 10        = 100

The student now has to understand the significance of the position of a figure in relation to hundreds, tens, and ones.

That is, for example, that 126 is composed of

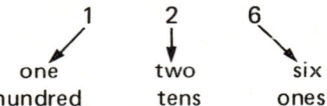

    1        2       6

  one     two     six
hundred  tens    ones

An additional problem at this stage can be the significance of a nought. At first, introduce the student to numbers with a nought at the end, eg 520.

The second stage is to introduce numbers with no tens, eg 502. Once the student is familiar with the significance of nought, various activities can be devised to reinforce his knowledge of place value.

eg  ●  Present the student with various numbers:

    507               254
        603   921
  920  266        630

Ask questions, such as,

Which numbers contain two tens?
Which numbers have no ones?
Which numbers have nine hundreds?
Which numbers have no tens?

Which is the largest number?
Which number is the nearest to 500?
Which is the smallest number?

    ●  To see if the student understands the value of numbers ask him to place these, or other numbers, in sequence, starting with the lowest and going upwards, or in the reverse order.

## 2.7.3 Simple addition of fractions

Although a student may not be able to manipulate fractions mathematically, he will be aware of them from various aspects of life,

eg ½ lb butter
½ pint of beer
¼ lb of tea

When introducing addition of fractions, it is this previous knowledge which should be used and built upon.

Use these simple fractions, and show how they are built up to form one whole, eg

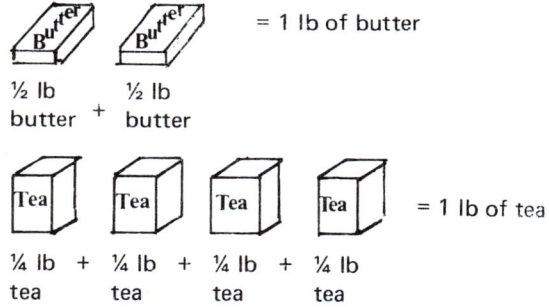

You can devise various ways to demonstrate the relationship between fractions and whole numbers.

● Use a strip of paper, folded to represent whichever fraction is being dealt with;

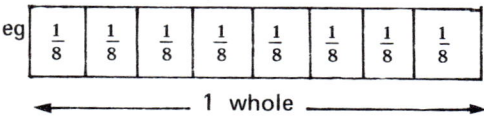

This simple apparatus can be used to show addition and subtraction of fractions.

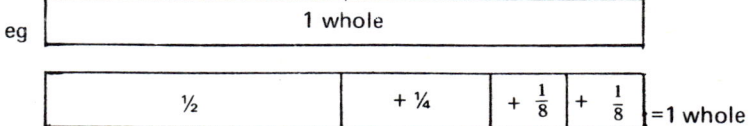

NB. In *Make it Count* Part 7, this is demonstrated by means of blocks. In this case the blocks are split into equal fractional parts.

Either of these methods can be used in addition and subtraction. If taught in appropriate groups, the apparatus can also be used to show the relationship between certain fractions.

If, for example, $\frac{1}{2}$  $\frac{1}{4}$  and $\frac{1}{8}$  are grouped together, it can

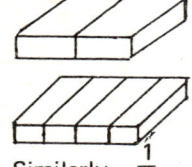

be shown that $\frac{4}{8} = \frac{2}{4} = \frac{1}{2}$

Similarly, $\frac{1}{3}$   $\frac{1}{6}$  and $\frac{1}{9}$   form an appropriate grouping, as also do $\frac{1}{5}$ and $\frac{1}{10}$

At this simple stage then, a number of addition and conversion sums can be done by the student, using the apparatus described.

## 2.7.4 Simple addition and subtraction of fractions and whole numbers

To begin with, restrict the addition of whole numbers and fractions to practical situations, familiar to the student. This would involve problems such as,

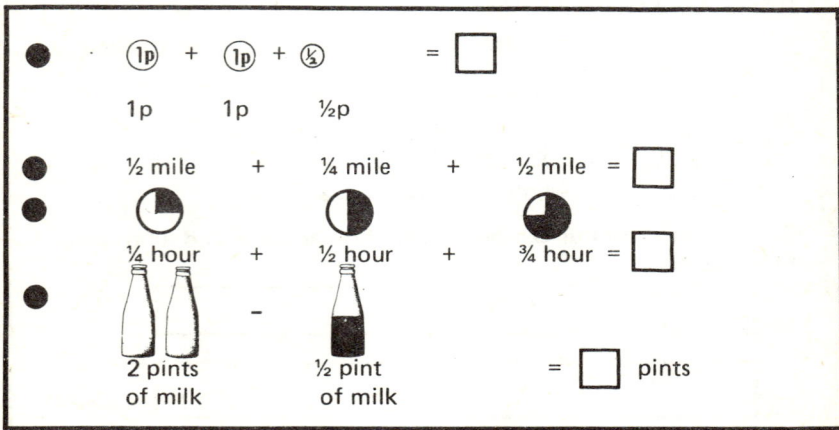

At this stage addition and subtraction of fractions should be confined to concrete examples. Indeed, with the introduction of decimalisation and metrication the necessity to perform complex operations involving fractions is decreasing.

## Section 2.8  Using numbers over 100 and introducing decimals

### 2.8.1  Addition, in hundreds

In section 2.4.2 we suggested how addition of tens and ones involving carrying could be explained to the student. When he is familiar with this work, you should introduce calculations involving hundreds.

---

Since the student is already acquainted with the idea of carrying from one column to another, he should not find too much difficulty in extending this to a further column (or indeed columns). Remember also that your student may need to be able to cope with a long list of figures (eg as in shopping bills) rather than numbers presented in two or three lines only.

---

### 2.8.2  Subtraction, in hundreds

As the student has already covered subtraction with decomposition from tens to ones, there should be little problem in applying this to larger numbers.

---

For the sake of simplicity it may be appropriate at first to restrict the decomposition to the hundreds column.

Give the student an example such as;

$$\begin{array}{r} 6\ 5\ 8 \\ -\ 2\ 9\ 4 \\ \hline \\ \hline \end{array}$$ and demonstrate that by taking a hundred from the hundreds column, this can be changed into 10 tens. Added to the 5 tens already present, this makes 15 tens, so enabling the subtraction to proceed.

When the student has learnt to cope successfully with this, decomposition of both tens and hundreds can be combined in the one calculation.

---

Perhaps the most complicated aspect of decomposition is when there is a nought involved.

eg

$$
\begin{array}{r}
^5\cancel{6}\,{}^9\cancel{0}\,{}^1 4 \\
-\ 2\ 8\ 7 \\
\hline
3\ 1\ 7
\end{array}
$$

Since 7 cannot be subtracted from 4, the student would normally transfer a ten to the ones column. When there are no tens however, he must first change a hundred into 10 tens, and then one of these tens into ten ones. Having dealt with these preliminaries, he can now proceed with the subtraction.

## 2.8.3 Multiplication, with answers in the hundreds

In Section 2.5.3 multiplication with carrying between the ones and tens column was discussed. Following on from this, discuss with the student how to extend carrying into the hundreds.

Give the student an example such as:

$$
\begin{array}{r}
6\ 8 \\
\times\ 4 \\
\hline
\end{array}
$$

From his previous experience, the student will be able to cope with multiplying a ones column where there is carrying into the tens. Similarly, he will now find that by multiplying the tens column, the answer is in the hundreds, and so needs to be written in a separate column.

As a check on the student's understanding of this, ask him to read back his answer. By asking him to do this, you will know whether the student is aware of the place value of each figure, and that being able to complete the sum successfully is not simply a matter of rote learning.

## 2.8.4 An introduction to decimals

As we stated earlier, one of the aims of this outline programme of work is to make the student aware of the relationship between various mathematical operations and concepts. Following this principle, this section is intended to show the connection between fractions and decimals. Decimalisation is best known to us through our money system. Therefore, calculations involving money provide the easiest introduction to decimals.

Taking as a basis the fact that £1 is composed of 100 pence, go on to explain that:

The decimal point denotes the division between pounds and pence, and that each of these pennies represents

$\dfrac{1}{100}$ of £1, or, £0·01.

£1 is made up of ten 10 pennies

That is, 10 pence is $\dfrac{1}{10}$ of £1, or £0·10

or £0·1

50p is ½ of £1, and is represented as £0·50

or £0·5

By using these commonest parts of a pound, the 1p, the 10p, and the 50p, the student should begin to understand in which way a decimal is part of a whole number. It is not necessary at this stage for the student to be able to convert less familiar fractions into decimals. Rather, the aim is that the student can recognise the relationship between fractions and decimals more commonly used.

## Section 2.9   Decimals and percentages

### 2.9.1  Concept of decimals

In *Make it Count* the work on decimals mostly concentrates on decimal money. Although a student may be very capable when dealing practically with money, make sure that he is equally aware of how it is represented in figures.

Through the work covered in the last section the student will already know certain decimals commonly in use, such as 50p represented as £0·50. It is important that he develops the ability to generalise his knowledge of decimals from the money system to other situations. By using the 100 square, it is possible to demonstrate to the student the meaning of decimals.

Taking as an example the number 4·37, explain to the student that the 4 represents 4 whole units, or 4 large squares. The ·37 can then be demonstrated by the small squares on the grid. 10 squares represent 0·10, 1 square represents 0·01. Therefore, the number 4·37 is represented as 4 complete squares, plus 37 small squares.

As well as the 100 square, a number line such as a 100 centimetre tape measure can be used to demonstrate the same idea.

N.B. Although a figure containing two places of decimals was chosen here as an example, student's work should initially be restricted to figures with only one decimal place, eg 4·3. For this, a strip divided into ten subdivisions would be sufficient to demonstrate its meaning.

## 2.9.2 Addition and subtraction of decimal money

There are many occasions when a student will need to be able to add up various amounts of money, the most obvious being in connection with bills. It is, therefore, most useful to explain the addition and subtraction of decimal money using examples directly relevant to the student, eg wage slip, bank statement, gas or electricity bill, etc.

| | |
|---|---|
| eg<br>£16·32<br>8·41<br>72·66<br>+    ·32<br>―――― | By now the student will know how to add up three or more columns of figures. Explain that the addition of decimals involves the same process, the only difference being that care must be taken with the positioning of the decimal point. Point out that the same applies for the subtraction of decimals. |

### 2.9.3 Percentages

Initially, an explanation of percentages can perhaps best be done by means of the 100 square. Use as a basis for work percentages which the student may already be familiar with, for example:

---

10% service charge on a menu,     7% interest at a bank,
   8% VAT on a bill,            20% off marked price in a sale,

Taking as the easiest example the 10% service charge, explain to the student what this would mean in terms of a bill for £1. Refer the student to a 100 square.

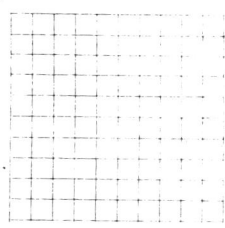

Explain that 1 square represents 1%.

In this case 1 square also represents 1 pence. Therefore 10% of £1 is 10 pence. The 10 pence is then added to the £1 to find the total amount charged.

---

Though the examples should be made increasingly more difficult, for basic numeracy it will probably be sufficient for most students to restrict calculations to finding percentages of units of 100. If, however, a student needs for some reason to go beyond this stage, this is probably the time when you can introduce the student to using a calculator (see *Make it Count* workbook).

### 2.9.4 Commonly used percentages

A number of students will find it useful to know what the most commonly used percentages mean in terms of fractions:

ie   10%   is the same as   $\frac{1}{10}$

     20%   is the same as   $\frac{1}{5}$

     25%   is the same as   $\frac{1}{4}$

$33\frac{1}{3}$% is the same as $\frac{1}{3}$

50%    is the same as $\frac{1}{2}$

75%    is the same as $\frac{3}{4}$

Since some of the above percentages are often seen in adverts announcing price reductions, it may be useful to use these as a basis for work.

## Section 2.10 More advanced multiplication and division

### 2.10.1 Long multiplication

Although a student will need to be able to deal with simple multiplication more frequently, there are situations where he will need to be able to cope with long multiplication. For example, this may be in connection with wages, or perhaps working out the total cost of hire-purchase repayments.

---

To begin with, it would be advisable to present an example of a multiplication sum with no carrying. The example chosen here is the second stage, where carrying has been introduced.

```
    2 7
  X 3 2
    5 4
  8 1 0
  8 6 4
```

Although it is possible to start multiplying by either the tens or the ones figure, it is probably easier for the student if he begins by multiplying the ones. By doing this, the first stage of the sum is exactly the same as he has been previously taught for simple multiplication.

When he comes to multiplying the tens figure, in this case the 3, make sure that he realises that it is 3 tens, and that he places the answer in the correct column.

---

When going on to multiplication in hundreds, precede the work by explaining to the student how to multiply by 100, ie by adding two noughts to the end of a number.

## 2.10.2 Multiplication of decimals

When learning multiplication of decimals, the student follows exactly the same procedure as for ordinary long multiplication. The only additional work is in the positioning of the decimal point. When calculating the sum ignore the decimal points. The student proceeds to multiply as normal. After he has arrived at the final answer, point out to him that this is where he returns to repositioning the decimal point. He does this by adding up the places of decimals after the decimal point in the original numbers and counts back the same number of decimal places before positioning the decimal point. Eg in the case of 2·7 X 3·2, there are two figures after the decimal point. Therefore the answer is 8·64.

## 2.10.3 Long division

When you first teach a student long division he may find the number of steps involved rather confusing. To overcome this, it may be helpful to list the processes involved, and to tell him that it is simply a matter of repeating these stages. Also, begin with sums that divide exactly, without remainders.

N.B. Since long division can be a complicated process, encourage the student to estimate the answer so that he has a means of checking his final answer.

Taking as an example:

```
      113
26 | 2938
     26
     ---
     33
     26
     --
     78
     78
```

Explain to the student how to follow the various steps:

(1) How many times does the divisor, 26, go into the first two figures, 29?
The answer is written *above* the second figure.

(2) The divisor is multiplied by this figure, and the answer written *below* the first two figures,

ie 1 X 26 = 26

(3) The 26 is subtracted from 29 and the result written below.

(4) The next figure is brought down alongside the 3, so creating the new number 33.

N.B. Point out to the student that at this stage the whole process begins again, and is repeated until the sum is completed.

## 2.10.4 Long division of decimals

Long division of decimals involves the same process as normal long division, except for the positioning of the decimal point.

eg

$2 \cdot 67 \overline{\smash) 29 \cdot 4}$

The divisor is made into a whole number.

In order to do this, the student must move the decimal point the appropriate number of places to the right, in the example 2 places. The same process must also be done to the number to be divided, so changing it in this example from 29·4 to 2940. The decimal point is then placed above the bracket in the correct position. The whole sum then has been altered before the division begins, and now reads as

$$267 \overline{\smash) 2940 \cdot}$$

The student then proceeds as for ordinary long division.

## Section 2.11 Graphs, areas and averages

(N.B. The work in this section refers to Part 12 of *Make it Count.*)

## 2.11.1 Graphs

Explain first to the student that graphs are a visual means of representing information of various kinds. It will help the student's understanding and interpretation of graphs if you help him to construct one himself.

To do this he will have to know: how to collect the information, what scale to choose, and what type of graph is best for the purpose.

Try to make the graph relevant to the interests of the student, and choose a subject where the information is easily available. Eg, the height and weight of members of his family, or the family size of a group of students. Show the student how to gather and record the information.

Having collected the information, next choose the scale. Explain the importance of using squared paper, and how this helps in determining the scale to be used. Initially it is easier if each square is chosen to represent one object.

Next draw the horizontal and vertical axis, and show the student how to label these.

Last, choose which type of graph to use, either a line or block graph. It is probably easier for the student to begin with a block graph. Show him how to fill in the information he has collected. Although we very rarely have to draw graphs, it is not infrequent that we need to read information from them. Therefore, use the graph the student produces and extract various pieces of information from it.

Having done a fairly simple graph with your student, progress to one where the scale is more complicated and the numbers involved larger. Explain to the student that a scale must be chosen which will include the highest and lowest figure on the graph. Also, emphasise that the scale is constant. Discuss what this scale will be, and how to arrange it on the squared paper.

As a comparison to the first example, perhaps choose to present the same information in the form of a line graph. Finally, always use the graph to read information contained in it. Also, present examples of graphs produced commercially, for the student to interpret.

## 2.11.2 Areas

Students are most likely to need area work for home requirements, such as buying a carpet, buying wood for shelving, or tiles for a wall. It is advisable, therefore, not to teach area work in the abstract, but to relate it to practical activities.

eg

Each tile is 10 cms by 10 cms

The wall is 90 cms by 50 cms

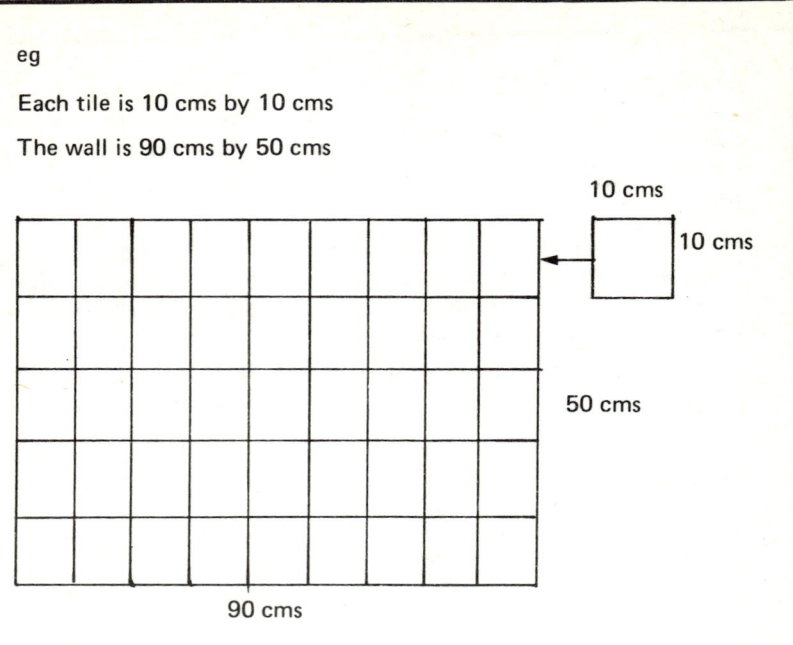

10 cms

10 cms

50 cms

90 cms

Draw this to scale and ask the student to work out how many tiles are needed to cover an area 90 X 50 cms. It is most likely that the student will reach the result by adding up the total number of squares. If this is so, point out the quicker method of multiplying the length of two adjacent sides.    An example similar to this would be finding the number of carpet squares that would fit into a room.

Carrying on from the idea of fitting squares into a space, the student should go on to finding area simply by the multiplication method. A check as to the accuracy of this can still be made by drawing the shape to scale, dividing it into appropriate squares, and adding these up.

## 2.11.3 Averages

As with other basic number work keep the examples as closely related to real life situations as possible. When you introduce averages to your student be sure not only to explain the concept, but also to demonstrate the calculations.

eg   the weekly wages of a group of men are;

£46, £32, £38 and £52.

Explain that the steps involved are;

1)   Add up the figures to find the total sum (ie £168)

2)   Divide this total by the number of figures (ie  4, the average wage being £42).

3)   Encourage your student to check the feasibility of his answer by seeing if it falls between the extremes of the largest and smallest numbers.

# PART III   CASE STUDIES

## Introduction

Part II consisted of an outline programme of tuition, but one expressed solely in terms of the basic number skills. As we stated at the beginning of this manual it illustrates one way of sequencing the learning of those skills. However, it would be a mistake to regard such an outline as the total programme in itself. It is no more than the skeleton upon which the flesh and blood of numeracy tuition, the work derived from the student's real needs and interests, is built. If you fail to relate the teaching of skills to the student's own needs the result can be boring rote work of the most off-putting kind.

It can, of course, be difficult at times to successfully marry the need for structure and practice with the need for relevance. Rather than attempt to strain this relationship and seek for trivial (or ludicrous!) connections, you may find it best to divide up lessons into shorter sections. Thus, part of the lesson could be devoted to working at the real mathematical problems your student faces and during the rest of the lesson attempt to develop his ability to perform particular skills by more formal practice.

In broad terms, it is possible either to teach the basic skills *through* consideration of the student's own particular needs and circumstances or, once having mastered these skills they can then be *applied* to everyday numeracy requirements. What is essential is that at some stage the learning programme which you and your student jointly devise, links together the basic skills within the broader context of his mathematical needs.

For example, your student may wish to be able to check bills and receipts but lack the ability to do the necessary addition. You can either teach him addition as a process in the abstract and then when he has mastered this, see if he can apply it to bills and receipts, or teach him addition by means of the bills, even though these would have to be simplified at first, you may then go on to see if he can apply his knowledge of addition to other situations. Either of these approaches is preferable to one which concentrates solely upon the skills to the exclusion of any practical application. However, wherever possible the latter approach (teaching the skills through the practical needs of the student) should be employed, because this effectively harnesses the interest of the student.

Of course, the mathematical needs of students vary considerably from individual to individual. This section of the manual is not intended as a blueprint for a syllabus. On the contrary, it is presented in the form of three case studies in order to emphasise the need for programmes of work to be tailor-made to the individual student. *They are not intended as syllabuses to be used with other students* but merely indicate the sort of mathematical work which can be derived from real life examples.

**Points to note**

- The work outlined in each case study is not presented in any particular sequence but divided into themes, eg numeracy at work, shopping, budgeting, etc. However, with a real student it is important to marry the sequential and functional aspects of the programme. Thus any particular theme which you use needs to be broken down into its constituent sub-skills.

  If you do not do this and a number of new teaching points are introduced simultaneously, the student will be confused. It is a relatively straightforward process to isolate the relevant sub-skills; for instance in the case of a time sheet a number of operations of varying complexity may be involved — subtraction and addition of time, multiplication or money (both whole numbers and decimals) multiplication involving fractions (eg: time and a half, time and a quarter). These need to be presented in an order which is compatible with the student's present ability. So if he is capable of addition and subtraction only concentrate on work using the time sheet which gives practice in those skills. Multiplication of whole numbers could be introduced later, before the multiplication of fractions and so on.

- The first case study, that of Colin, is presented in greater detail and reproduces examples of work to show you the kinds of specific teaching materials which can quickly and easily be made for individual students. The other two case studies of Jean and George serve the same purpose but are much briefer.

## 3.1 Case study 1: Colin

Colin Dale is 32 and married with three children. For the last five years he has worked in a textile mill as a machine operator. Recently, he was offered promotion to supervisor but refused because he felt he could not cope with the time sheets and the simple monitoring of materials used on the section. He sought help with numeracy specifically to enhance his job prospects.

He is interested in motoring and wishes to sell his car and buy another in the near future. He is also keen on do-it-yourself and enjoys doing jobs about the house.

Colin can manage to do calculations using addition and subtraction but only if the numbers involved are small and even then he works very slowly. Beyond this his mathematical ability is very limited. He will need to improve his speeds as well as general level of ability if he is ever to cope as a supervisor.

On the following pages there are a series of worksheets designed specifically for Colin. They are not meant to be reproduced as they stand, but illustrate the range of topics which can be developed for an individual student. Alongside these there are more general notes suggesting ways in which similar work can be done with other students. The worksheets are not presented in order of difficulty, but by topic, eg at work, travelling, etc.

### 3.1.1 At work: time sheets

As supervisor, Colin would need to be able to calculate the time worked by a particular person, and how much they earned.

This is one particular example, which could be used to show how these calculations are made.

**Sample of possible work**

## TIME SHEET

| Day | : Checked | | Checked | | Hours Daily total |
|-----|-----|-----|-----|-----|-----|
| | In | Out | In | Out | |
| Mon. | 8.00 | 12.00 | 1.00 | 4.00 | |
| Tues. | 9.00 | 12.00 | 1.00 | 4.30 | |
| Wed. | 8.30 | 12.00 | 1.30 | 5.00 | |
| Thur. | 9.00 | 12.30 | 1.30 | 5.00 | |
| Fri. | 8.00 | 12.00 | 1.00 | 4.30 | |
| Sat. | 8.30 | 12.00 | | | |
| Total hours | | | | | |
| Rate of pay: £1·50 an hour | | | | | |
| Total wage | | | | | |

The aim of this example would be to introduce addition of time, and show Colin how to add up the daily, and weekly number of hours worked.

Having done that, he can then go on to work out the weekly wage. Once this idea has been established, then the idea of time and a half, double time, etc could be introduced.  For example:

**Sample of possible work**

Stan is a spinner.
He earns £2·00 an hour.
He works 9 hours a day, 5 days a week.
He works 2 hours overtime on Thursday.
For this he earns time and a half.
How much does he earn?

## 3.1.2 At work: monitoring materials

**Sample of possible work**

One of Colin's jobs as supervisor would be to calculate the number of bales of fibre used on his section. This chart shows the number used during a certain week.

| Days | Red | Yellow | Blue | Black | Green |
|------|-----|--------|------|-------|-------|
| Mon. | 75 | 49 | 52 | 62 | 73 |
| Tues. | 82 | 96 | 86 | 59 | 85 |
| Wed. | 65 | 57 | 75 | 44 | 96 |
| Thur. | 49 | 82 | 81 | 53 | 54 |
| Fri. | 60 | 94 | 74 | 64 | 87 |
| Sat. | 35 | 29 | 31 | 19 | 24 |

**Cost of bales**

| 10 bales of red | £29·00 |
|-----------------|--------|
| 10 bales of yellow | £26·00 |
| 10 bales of blue | £28·00 |
| 10 bales of black | £25·00 |
| 10 bales of green | £27·00 |

How many blue bales were used during the week?

Which colour was used the most, which the least?

On which day were the most bales used?

On which day the least used?

How much did the red bales cost for Friday?

The work presented here involves the ability to add up a list of figures.

This can prove a long and tedious task unless the student is taught how to add numbers quickly.

For example, present him with the sum

$$
\begin{array}{r}
14 \\
29 \\
36 \\
+\ 11 \\
\hline
\\
\hline
\end{array}
$$

show him how to add in number bonds of ten. The ability to do this will increase a student's speed and make him more aware of the relationship between numbers.

Adding up a list of numbers calls for great accuracy but equally important is the ability to estimate, eg what is the cost of 48 bales at £25·00 for 10? This involves the rounding off of numbers to the nearest 10, and then doing a quick multiplication to assess the approximate price of goods.

It should be impressed upon the student that although estimating foregoes some accuracy for speed, it can be extremely useful in many everyday situations.

A method which incorporates both speed and accuracy is using a calculator. If there is one available to a student, it can prove very useful to him to know how it works, so that he can both work out calculations, and check results already reached.

### 3.1.3 Note to tutors on how to make use of the student's work for teaching purposes

In this section on work, we have set out the problems relevant to one particular student. The work place however, provides endless possibilities for mathematical calculations, either simple or complex to suit the ability of each student. Thus, for example, wages can be looked at in the following ways:

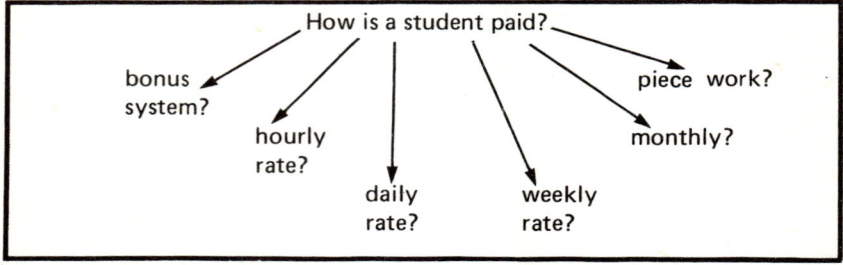

All of these rates are calculated in a different way. Does the student know how to calculate his?

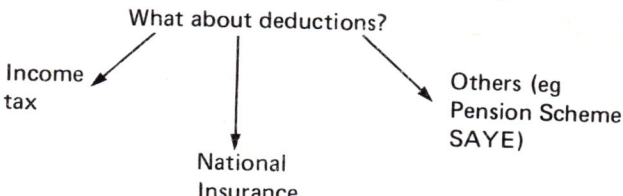

How do we work out how much tax we pay?

What *percentage* of our wages goes on deductions?

What is the difference between gross and nett pay?

To enable you to utilise other specific aspects of the work situation it is *essential* you discuss with your student the exact nature of his particular job, and draw your examples from his experience.

## 3.1.4 Travelling

Colin does a good deal of travelling by car. During the week he uses it mainly for journeys to work. He does, however, have the alternative of going by bus. Because of rising costs, Colin wanted to find out the relative price of both forms of transport. These are the calculations involved.

**Sample of possible work**

---

If he goes by car

Petrol costs 75p per gallon.

His car does 30 miles to the gallon.

He travels 6 miles to work.

How much does this journey cost him?

Coming back in the evening, Colin gives a friend a lift home. He pays half the cost of the petrol. How much does this journey cost him?

How much do the two journeys cost him each day?

---

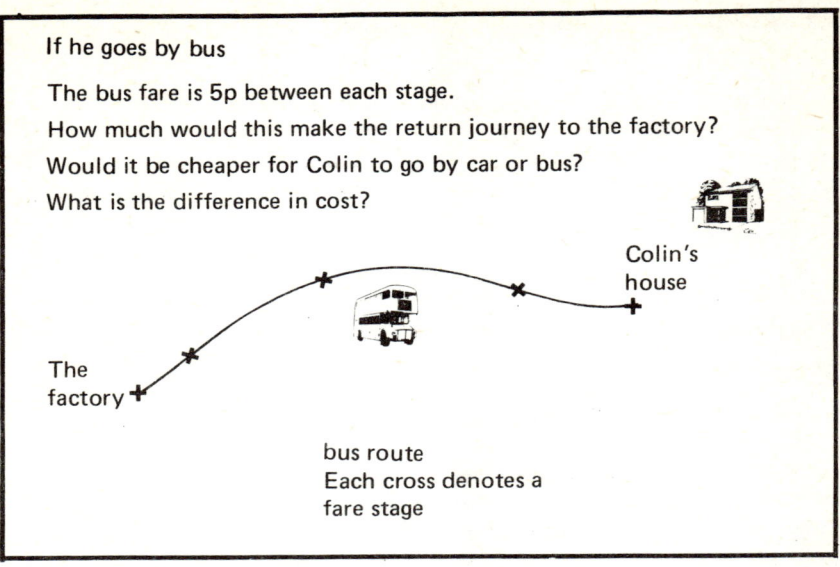

If he goes by bus

The bus fare is 5p between each stage.

How much would this make the return journey to the factory?

Would it be cheaper for Colin to go by car or bus?

What is the difference in cost?

Colin's house

The factory

bus route
Each cross denotes a
fare stage

Because he is a car owner, Colin is basically interested in travelling costs related to motoring. In the sample work sheet we have dealt solely with the cost of his travelling to work, but further calculations could come from working out the amount of petrol used during weekend journeys, car maintenance costs, and the mileage done during holiday travel, etc.

Many students, however, will be more dependent on public transport, and will therefore be more concerned with the cost of daily bus or train journeys. For students with very basic numeracy needs, some work should therefore be done on simple addition of money, and the checking of change. The calculation of return and half fares and weekly, monthly or yearly season tickets may also be relevant to their needs.

For a student going on holiday, or undertaking a long journey, you can make a comparison between bus and train travel. The timetables will show comparative times of journeys, and are very useful in teaching addition and subtraction of time. The fares can be obtained from the railway station and the bus company and these can be used in teaching percentages, eg: midweek return or excursion rates compared to the standard fare.

## 3.1.5 Going on holiday

**Sample of possible work**

Colin and his family have 2 weeks' holiday. He wants to go to Spain, but doesn't know if he can afford it. He works out the cost of a holiday abroad, compared to a holiday in Britain.

### Holiday in Spain

For 14 days' Full Board the cost is £140.

Child reductions are ¼ off this price.

How much would it cost for him, his wife, and 3 children?

### Holiday in Britain

For 14 days in Bed and Breakfast accommodation it would cost £4 each night for each adult, ½ price for each child.

Colin thinks he would drive approximately 200 miles.

Petrol is 75p per gallon.

His car does 30 miles to the gallon.

On top of this Colin thinks they would spend at least £10 a day on food.

About how much would this holiday cost?

The mathematics involved in the sample of work illustrated includes multiplication, addition of money, and division related to fractions. This particular example is quite complicated since it arises from a real situation. It can provide the basis for a great deal of work.

Similar calculations for your student can be extended in a number of ways and possibly include aspects such as comparisons between the cost and time of travelling by different forms of transport, and the budgeting of spending money. Similarly, much work can derive from the cost of eating out. Whenever possible, try to use realistic prices in the calculations, though you may have to round off figures, for the sake of simplicity. *The important point is that the student recognises the kind of operation that he needs to perform when presented with such problems.*

## 3.1.6 Money matters

**Sample of possible work**

Colin and his wife want to buy a new car. They sell their old car to a garage and buy a newer one.

They get £850 for their old car.

The new one costs £1,500 on H.P.

What is the difference in price?

Colin pays back the difference at a rate of £10 a week.

How long does he take to pay it back?

Colin also wants a colour TV.

The TV costs £260 if he pays cash.

Colin gets the TV on H.P.

He pays £6 a week for 50 weeks.

How much does the TV cost him now?

**Further suggestions**

The idea of H.P. can lead on to interest rates and percentages. (You should always point out to your student that all forms of credit involve the payment of interest charges. These may be specified or added on to the cost indirectly.)

These examples are just two ways in which problems relating to money can be introduced. There are many other areas that can be covered: eg

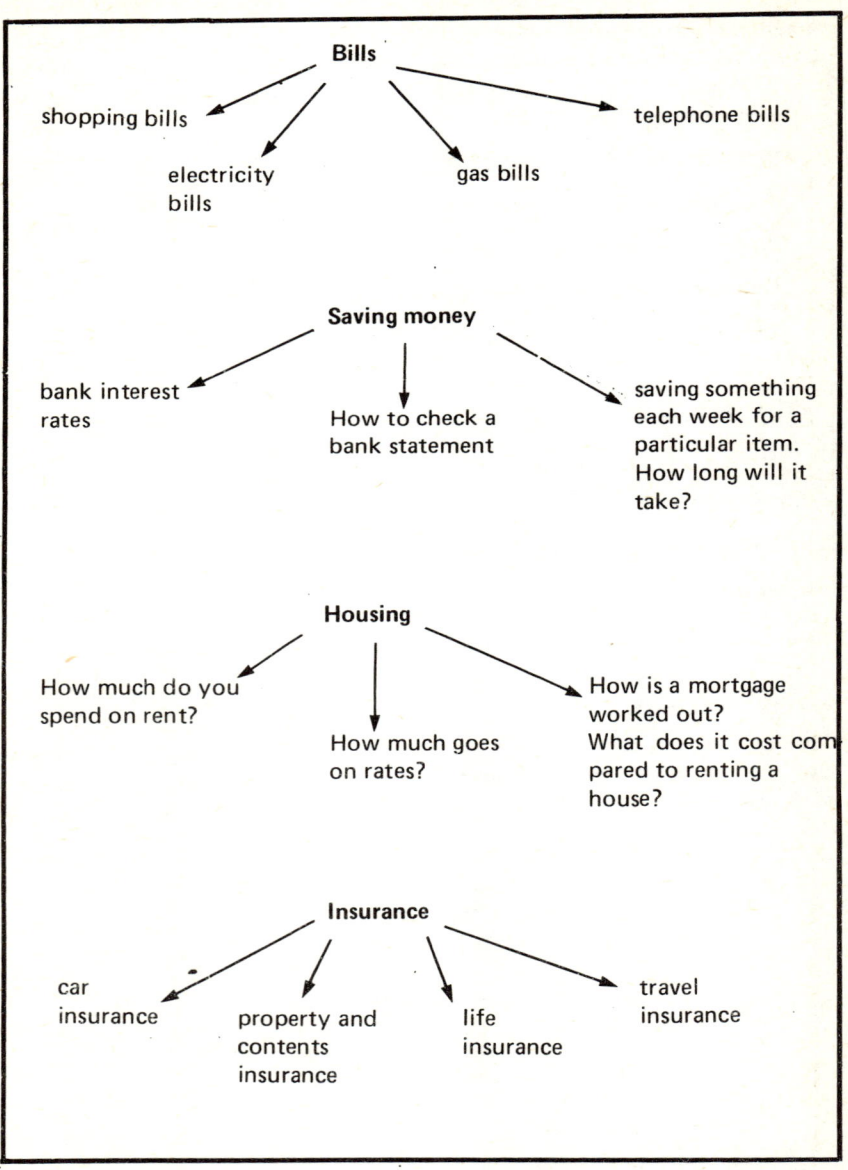

**Bills**

shopping bills

electricity
bills

gas bills

telephone bills

**Saving money**

bank interest
rates

How to check a
bank statement

saving something
each week for a
particular item.
How long will it
take?

**Housing**

How much do you
spend on rent?

How much goes
on rates?

How is a mortgage
worked out?
What does it cost com
pared to renting a
house?

**Insurance**

car
insurance

property and
contents
insurance

life
insurance

travel
insurance

## 3.1.7 Interests and hobbies

Colin is interested in do-it-yourself. To decorate a room he needs to be able to do the following calculations.

**Sample of possible work**

### For the wallpaper

The height of the wall is 8 feet.

Each roll of wallpaper is 33 feet long.

How many strips of wallpaper will be get from each roll?

Each roll of wallpaper costs £2·45.

If he needs 4 rolls how much will this cost? '

He needs two tins of paint, each costing £2·75.

What is the total cost of the paint and wallpaper?

5 yards

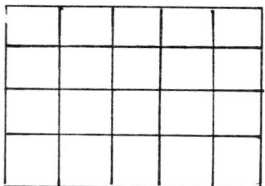

4 yards

Now he has decorated the room, Colin and his wife decide to buy a new carpet. Their room measures 5 X 4 yards. The carpet costs £2·50 a square yard. How much will it cost them?

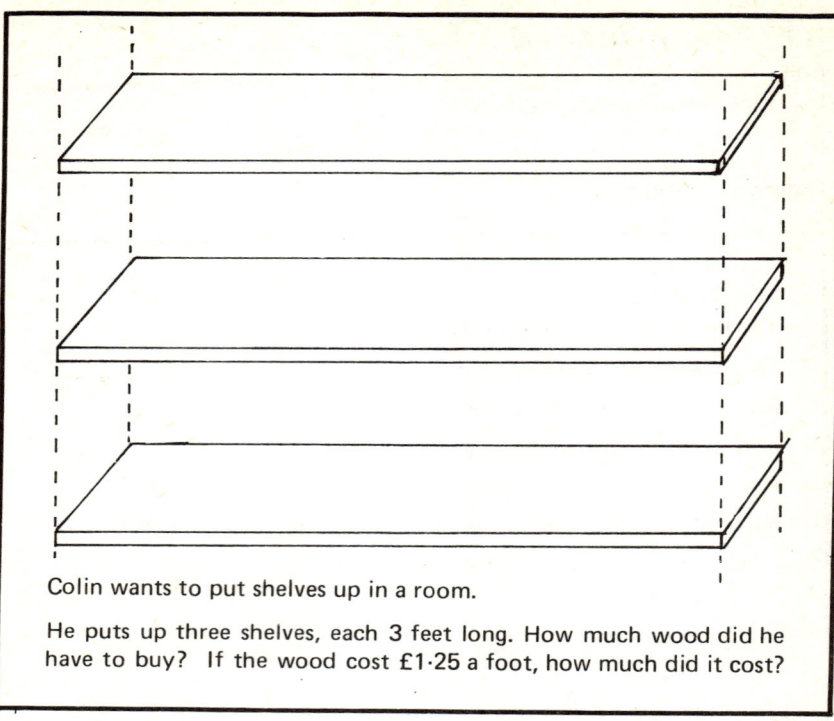

Colin wants to put shelves up in a room.

He puts up three shelves, each 3 feet long. How much wood did he have to buy? If the wood cost £1·25 a foot, how much did it cost?

Maths involved in the examples includes:

Division

Multiplication

Addition

Simple area work.

**Suggestions for tutors**

The ideas presented in this section are intended to show the type of work that can evolve out of a student's interests. The activities involved in D.I.Y. present endless teaching possibilities. However, any hobby or interest can provide a good basis for work. Specialist magazines and adverts can be very useful in supplying current prices and ideas, so that the mathematical work arising from this is realistic.

## 3.2 Case study 2: Jean

Jean Jones is a mother of three small children, the eldest of whom has just started school. Jean left school when she was fifteen, eight years ago, without taking any exams. She says that she was not interested in school work and truanted frequently. Her husband has recently left her and she feels she must get a job to support her family. During the interview she stated that she had difficulty with reading and writing too. In fact, she can read nothing but the simplest words. Although she can add up small numbers in her head quite quickly and accurately, she has great difficulty in writing them down, and often reverses the numerals, not only writing '72' for '27', but also 'ꓶ' for 'Ꮀ' and 'P' for 'ꟼ'.

As can be seen from the brief case study outline above Jean has quite severe learning difficulties. A programme of work must be devised which:

- attempts to supply information to help her make decisions, eg in relation to job applications.

- systematically develops the basic number skills within the context of her needs.

- takes into account her poor literacy ability.

In fact as much as possible of the learning programme would be derived from practical problems, and with the close co-operation of a literacy teacher both skills would be taught side-by-side. The following pages outline some of the activities which could be used as a starting point for the numeracy work.

## 3.2.1 Shopping

One of Jean's main concerns is with shopping. Living on a limited budget, Jean has to spend her money carefully. She has trouble adding up a bill, and often misses useful bargain offers because she cannot work out the savings involved. Also, since she cannot estimate the cost of a number of items, she is not sure when she goes out if she has enough money with her to cover her shopping bill.

Here are some suggestions for helping Jean (and others in a similar position) to cope with these shopping problems.

**Sample of possible work**

- Adding up shopping bills. Start at first with a small list of items —

  | eg | tea | 28p | Gradually increase the complexity of the |
  |---|---|---|---|
  | | bread | 15p | calculations. Supermarket checkout bills |
  | | jam | 25p | can be used as a basis for this work. |

- Checking change. Begin with a small sum of money, eg a newspaper costs 8p, how much change is there from 10p?

  The sum involved can be increased to 20p, 50p, £1, etc.

- Estimating the total cost of items, eg if Jean has 50p, will she have enough to buy a tin of pears at 28p and a bar of soap costing 11p?

- Calculating multiples of a certain sum, eg if 1 lb of potatoes costs 7p, what do 5 lb cost?

- Recognising bargains. Bargains take a variety of forms.

  (a) Price reductions    eg  '6p off' a bar of soap, originally 20p.
  Occasionally this involves fractions, eg

  half price

  (b) Bulk purchase    eg  multiples, such as,
  1 tin of soup costs 14p
  2 tins for 25p

  *or*  1 pack of sweets costs 8p
  5 packs cost 37p

*or* a comparison of weights,

eg ¼ lb of coffee costs £1·18

½ lb of coffee costs £2·20

All these involve calculating the amount saved.

## 3.2.2 Other ways of purchasing

Because of her financial circumstances, Jean often cannot afford to buy larger items such as clothing and household goods, outright. Therefore, she often makes use of other forms of purchasing which spread the payments over a longer period.

**Sample of possible work**

(a) A mail order club.

Jean pays 5p weekly for each £1 of the purchase price. She has bought a winter coat and a pair of shoes for one of her children at a total cost (including interest) of £12.

How much will she pay per week?

How many weeks will it take her to pay for the goods?

What will be balance owing be after five weeks?

| Date | Cost of foods | Weekly payments | Amount paid | Balance owing |
|------|---------------|-----------------|-------------|---------------|
| March 1st | £12 | 60p | £0·60 | £11·40 |
| March 8th | | 60p | £1·20 | £10·80 |
| March 15th | | | | |

(b) A shopping club

She has also joined a Christmas Club, at her local butcher, she is saving 15p a week.

How much will she have saved after 8 weeks?

There are 20 weeks to Christmas, how much will she be able to spend at Christmas?

(c) Hire-Purchase

This involves calculating the total cost of weekly instalments, compared to the original cost of an item to see how much extra is being paid.

 Jean wants to buy a radio, the cash price is £25.

She pays £5 deposit, then hire-purchase payments of 55p a week for 40 weeks.

How much has the radio finally cost her?

Discussions could be broadened out into a consideration of the advantages and disadvantages of H.P. compared with paying cash.

Rather than use artificial examples, it is *far* better to work directly from the student's real situation, and by so doing both teach the skills needed and supply the answer to particular problems he or she may have. However, where more practice is needed introduce further examples relating them as closely as possible to your student's experience.

### 3.2.3 Budgeting

Jean finds it increasingly difficult to make her money last out the week. She would like to know if there are any economies she can make, and would appreciate some help in budgeting her weekly money.

**Sample of possible work**

**Budgeting**

(a)  The cost of meals.

Because of lack of time Jean is often tempted to buy frozen and convenience foods rather than cook a meal using fresh materials. It may be possible to work out a comparison between the cost of making a meal at home  eg  a shepherd's pie using 1 lb of mince and 1 lb of potatoes (not forgetting to add in fuel costs etc), and the ready-made equivalent, a frozen shepherd's pie.

(b) Making your own clothes compared to buying them.

Jean is interested in dressmaking and wants to work out the comparative costs of making and buying a dress.

Further maths work would involve measuring and purchasing materials.

c) Paying bills.

Jean sometimes falls behind with bills and it is difficult to catch up with payments. Budgeting out a weekly sum of money may be helpful in overcoming this situation. You can help her to work out how much she needs to pay for rent, heating and fares, etc and convert this into a weekly amount. Also, help can be given in calculating particular bills,

eg the milk bill. Jean has two pints a day: experience can be given in counting in two's, then calculating the bill.

Jean pays her rent weekly. You can show her how the rent is calculated, and how much is due if she does fall into arrears eg

| Date | Rent | Rates | Total due | Money paid | Arrears |
|------|------|-------|-----------|------------|---------|
| 19th April | £5.00 | £2.00 | £7.00 | £7.00 | |
| 26th April | £5.00 | £2.00 | £7.00 | | £7.00 |
| 3rd May | £5.00 | £2.00 | £14.00 | £14.00 | |

Calculations can be based on rents and arrears.

## 3.2.4 Decisions

Jean is contemplating applying for a job as a cleaner for five hours a day. She is obviously concerned about whether it would be financially beneficial for her to take such a job.

The task involved has two aspects.

First, to find out the information relating to:

Hourly rate of pay.

Cost of transport to and from work.

Cost of a child minder.

Loss of Social Security benefits, etc.

And, second, to make the relevant mathematical calculations.

Because of Jean's difficulties in both numeracy and literacy such a complicated task could be very daunting. Although a whole programme of work can be developed from such a problem, it is obviously crucial that in the short term Jean receives immediate information to enable her to make a decision.

The number work involved can then be more thoroughly explained at a rate appropriate to Jean's ability.

## 3.3 Case study 3: George

George Fraser is twenty years old. He got married a year ago. His wife, Sue, is now expecting a baby and has given up her job as a hairdresser. At present they live with his parents but they would like to buy a house if possible. George works as a painter and decorator with a small firm but would eventually like to be self-employed.

George is a keen soccer fan and plays for a local amateur side. He also enjoys going out with his mates for a drink.

At the initial interview George stated that he had no difficulty with 'simple sums' but needed help with fractions and decimals. Subsequent lessons revealed, however, that although he could do simple written calculations he could not do them without putting them down on paper.

The following pages outline three aspects of the programme of work designed by George and his tutor.

## 3.3.1 Social interests

Once a week, George goes out with his three friends. Usually they go for a drink, and often have a game of darts in the pub. These activities include some maths work. Other social interests can also be used to introduce maths. If your student has any special interests, try to utilise them in some way.

## Sample of possible work

### Going to the pub

This can be the basis for work on addition, subtraction, multiplication and division. George and his friends decide to contribute to a kitty to buy the drinks for the evening. They each put in £1. George buys the first round of drinks, 4 pints of beer at 33p per pint.

How much did the round cost?

How much is left in the kitty? etc.

### Playing darts

Obviously number work is important in the game. It is a situation where the need for both *speed* and *accuracy* is vital. The game involves working out double and treble numbers, as well as a good deal of addition and subtraction and division by 2. If there is a darts board available, try this lesson out practically.

## Suggestions for other possible activities

### Dominoes

This game can be used in the early stages of numeracy in matching the same numbers, or adding up the dots.

### Bingo

This can be used for recognition of numbers, eg a student has one or two cards and has to cover up the numbers as called. This is very valuable in teaching place value.

### Cards

Again, this can be used for the recognition of numbers and/or addition.

### Going to the cinema or a disco

Working out the cost of entrance, fares to and from, what is spent when you are there?

*Always try to use your student's own interests as a basis for his mathematical work.*

### 3.3.2 Sports

George is very interested in football. Not only does he support his home team, he also plays for a local club.

It is probable that a number of students will be interested in football. If not, there may be some other sport in which they participate. The following is a brief sample of the mathematical work which can derive from these activities.

**Sample of possible work**

---

**Football**

Use football pools to add up points.

If a person either follows a particular club, or plays for an amateur team, that specific team can be used in a number of ways, eg

> adding up their points.
>
> total number of goals scored.
>
> working out the number of goals scored, by the team over several matches or in a season.
>
> how many goals scored *against* a team.
>
> a graph to show the number of spectators at each match.
>
> a graph to show the number of goals scored by each team member.
>
> the total of goals at home and away.
>
> the cost of players.

**Cricket**

Given a copy of the scores of a particular team, questions could be based on:—

> who scored the most runs.
>
> what was the total number of runs.
>
> batting averages.

**Horse Racing**

> Working out betting odds.
>
> Calculating winnings.

---

### 3.3.3 Taking decisions

George is contemplating taking two major decisions:

- buying a house

- becoming self-employed

Moreover his financial position has changed dramatically because his wife is no longer working.

To be able to take informed decisions, George needs to be aware of the financial implications. A major part of his learning programme would be centred around these mathematical calculations and wherever possible the basic number skills taught through these real life examples. For instance, a great deal of maths work could derive from George contemplating whether or not to buy a house. Areas that could be investigated include:

a)   purchase price of house

b)   mortgage repayments

c)   rates

d)   legal and other fees

e)   cost of moving

f)   tax relief on mortgage

g)   comparison with present rent

h)   cost of furnishing and equipping a house

i)   cost of repairs.

## Concluding remarks

Any manual in this field cannot hope to be comprehensive or to be of equal relevance to all tutors. We have written it in the hope that it will raise the issue of training and support in numeracy tuition; it is not intended to provide definitive answers. It has been written to accompany both the *Make it Count* workbook (the sequence of part II of the manual follows the sequence of the workbook) and the pack produced for trainers. We hope you have been able to read the manual while attending a training course so that many of the points raised can be discussed more thoroughly. We would appreciate your comments; it is only by getting feedback from you, the tutors, that we can develop and improve the manual . Send them to the Courses Editor, National Extension College, 131 Hills Road, Cambridge, CB2 1PD.
We have emphasised:

- Numeracy is a practical skill. As adults we need to be numerate for specific purposes. Tutoring is more effective if it is related to the individual student's needs than if number skills are taught as abstract processes.

- Tutors should encourage their students to continue their learning independently eg: to practise their maths when they are 'out and about' for example by adding up car numbers or multiplying the numbers on bus tickets etc.

- Maths has an internal logic and structure. Tutoring should reflect this and marry it with the practical needs of students.

- Effective tutoring of adults is to a large extent a matter of getting away from a school teacher/pupil relationship and creating an appropriate working relationship between *equals*.

- As with any teaching it is important to plan and prepare lessons in advance while at the same time remaining sufficiently flexible to take advantage of new topics which can be used for teaching as they arise.

Finally, we would like to stress, once again, that this manual can provide no more than a set of starting points. We would encourage you to combine it with any training provided locally, and to periodically review, with your student, the nature of the work upon which you are engaged.

We would like to wish you every success with your teaching.